NOT TO THE STRONG

NOT TO THE STRONG

ELWOOD McQUAID

The Friends of Israel Gospel Ministry, Inc.
P. O. Box 908, Bellmawr, New Jersey 08099

NOT TO THE STRONG

©Copyright 1991

The Friends of Israel Gospel Ministry, Inc.
Bellmawr, New Jersey 08099

Printed in the United States of America
Library of Congress Catalog Card Number: 91-71438
ISBN 0-915540-45-2

The Friends of Israel Gospel Ministry, Inc.
P. O. Box 908, Bellmawr, New Jersey 08099

With God there are no extraordinary people—only ordinary ones through whom He chooses to do extraordinary things.

And what shall I more say?
For the time would fail me to tell
of Gideon, and of Barak, and of Samson, and of Jephthah . . .
Who, through faith, subdued kingdoms,
wrought righteousness, obtained promises,
stopped the mouths of lions,
Quenched the violence of fire,
escaped the edge of the sword,
out of weakness were made strong.
Hebrews 11:32-34

CONTENTS

Introduction

THE PEOPLE WHOSE STORIES are told in the Book of Judges are magnificent examples of His ability to take the most common among us and "from weakness" create giants in the faith.

The period of the judges was a time of national failure, spiritual disintegration, and moral decay. It was, in fact, a time startlingly reminiscent of our own. As the four *deliverers* found in Hebrews chapter 11 *Hall of Heroes* are brought before us, we can anticipate a collective expression of surprise. They were, to the man, plagued with problems—cut-from-clay illustrations of Alfred Edersheim's candid observation, "The Judges were Israel's representative men—representative of its faith and hope, but also of its sin and decay."

But they were not Israel's men only, for the lessons to be learned from their lives transcend time or place. These are our men too—yours and mine—people through whom God wants to say something to us, something that will instill an understanding of life's hard realities, our potential for God, and His faithful provision, which can make us consistent overcomers.

Not To The Strong is not, therefore, a commentary on the Book of Judges. It is a study in lives—lives in which problems

1

are solved and victories won, but lives that see new problems growing out of their initial conquests. These must also be dealt with.

The message is not complicated but simple—simple to the point of contradicting our habit of clouding issues by inventing formulas and systems that make triumphant Christian living much more complicated than God ever intended it to be. The instructions and admonitions coming to us through these men relate to two basic words—words, as we shall see, that each of us needs to hear again and again.

We will find our own reflections as we study *Barak—The Faceless; Gideon—The Fearful; Jephthah—The Forsaken; Samson—The Failure.*

The Man	The Problem	The Method of Victory Divine Side	Human Side	The Outgrowth Problem	The Abiding Solution
Barak	Faceless (Judges 4)	Direct divine intervention *Rain and Flood* (Judges 5:4,20–21)	Faith and Obedience	Pride Song (Judges 5)	Remembrance (Eph. 2:11–13)
Gideon	Fearful (Judges 6:1–7,14)	Applying a Divine strategy *Lamps and Pitchers* (Judges 7)	Faith and Obedience	Human Wisdom (Judges 8:22–35)	Reliance (James 1:5)
Jephthah	Forsaken (Judges 11:1–3)	Spirit Empowered Confrontation (Judges 11:4–33)	Faith and Obedience	Impulsive Promise *Vow* (Judges 11:30–40)	Reservation (James 1:19)
Samson	Failure (Judges 13:1–16,31)	Divine Strength (Judges 16:22–30)	Faith and Obedience	Terminal *Forfeited life* (Judges 16:23–31)	Resolution (Eph. 5:14–17)

1

In the Grasp of Failure

JOSHUA WAS DEAD. For years thereafter, gray-haired elders spent their evenings relating stories of their glory days at the side of the incomparable commander-in-chief of an infant nation. Wide-eyed youngsters, hurried off to bed by watchful Jewish mothers, slipped into sleep to the accompaniment of fanciful visions of someday becoming a new Joshua in Israel.

But the old men were all gone now, and with them in their sepulchers the burning resolve to capture all the land promised to Abraham and his posterity was laid to rest. Indeed, as we read the Book of Judges, we must be astonished at the swiftness with which the rising generation had forsaken their singular position in the program of God.

"And also all that generation were gathered unto their fathers: and there arose another generation after them, who knew not the LORD, nor yet the works which he had done for Israel" (Jud. 1:10).

Joshua had led Abraham's descendants into the land amid towering prospects of their becoming a nation the like of which the world had never seen. They were destined to be a people ruled by God, witnessing to divine truth and carrying the seed of the promised Redeemer of mankind. Sadly, that generation would fall far short of honoring their commission.

The miraculous deliverance from the brick kilns of Egypt, the experiences of the wilderness wanderings, passing the Jordan into the promised land, and the unprecedented victory at Jericho were all ancient history. None of these experiences seemed to hold any relevant application to their lives or times. They had lost all perspective of their peculiar relationship to Jehovah and the position in future history to be occupied by the nation. The words of Moses in his parting address to the people had been relegated to the musty recesses of the historical archives. In short, they had lost their sense of mission. The disciplined warrior nation, which had entered Canaan with such high expectations, had disintegrated into quarrelsome tribal factions. Their view of the common goals to which this theocratic people were committed had degenerated to the point that they were as likely to make war with one another as with the enemies of Israel.

Why?

How could a people with such magnificent prospects fall so far? Divine direction had been specific. They were fearlessly to invade the land and drive out the interlopers who occupied the country God had given the Jewish people in perpetuity. Their victory had already been assured. Jehovah's arm of strength had been bared on their behalf too many times to leave them in doubt. The Lord had promised; He would perform. It was as simple as that. The message to Moses' successor, Joshua, was clear:

> Moses, my servant, is dead; now therefore arise, go over this Jordan, thou and all this people, unto the land which I do give to them, even to the children of Israel. Every place that the sole of your foot shall tread upon, that have I given unto you, as I said unto Moses. From the wilderness and this Lebanon even unto the great river, the river Euphrates, all the land of the Hittites, and unto the Great Sea toward the going down of the sun, shall be your border. There

shall not any man be able to stand before thee all the days of thy life. As I was with Moses, so I will be with thee; I will not fail thee, nor forsake thee. Be strong and of good courage; for unto this people shalt thou divide for an inheritance the land which I swore unto their fathers to give them. Only be thou strong and very courageous, that thou mayest observe to do according to all the law, which Moses, my servant, commanded thee; turn not from it to the right hand or to the left, that thou mayest prosper wherever thou goest (Josh. 1:2-7).

Moses had assured them of God's pledge of His presence, power, and provision: "The LORD thy God, he will go over before thee, and he will destroy these nations from before thee, and thou shalt possess them; and Joshua, he shall go over before thee, as the LORD hath said" (Dt. 31:3).

They were to possess the land through a step-by-step program of occupation. Actually, only a fraction of the promised territory was settled at the time of the judges. Again we must raise the question, Why?

A Chronicle of Defeat

The opening chapters of the Book of Judges provide dismal reading. There is a recurring cycle of failure followed by defeat. Seven times over we read the phrase, "And the children of Israel did evil in the sight of the LORD" (Jud. 2:11; 3:7, 12 (twice), 4:1; 6:1; 10:6).

An examination of these early chapters gives a clear diagnosis of Israel's problems and reveals exactly how they reached the low spiritual level occupied in the days of the judges. It is a valuable study, for by exploring the factors resident in Israel's failure, we can discover parallels often found in our own lives. And, after all, learning why we have failed is as important as discovering what we should do about it. As a matter of fact, it is an essential prerequisite to consistent spiritual living.

7

Incomplete Obedience

The first two chapters of Judges reveal the nation's growing proclivity for leaving things undone. God had instructed them to drive out the inhabitants of the land. As we shall see later, there were sound reasons for their doing this. Coexistence with people who were committed to their defeat simply could not be tolerated. Although they may not have understood all of the reasons for what they were doing, it was essential for them to follow instructions.

We read, however, "but [they] could not drive out the inhabitants of the valley, because they had chariots of iron" (Jud. 1:19).

"And the children of Benjamin did not drive out the Jebusites, who inhabited Jerusalem" (Jud. 1:21).

"Neither did Manasseh drive out the inhabitants of Beth-shean" (Jud. 1:27).

In six additional instances (Jud. 1:28, 29, 30, 31, 32, 33) Israel's failure to obey the divine dictate is solemnly unfolded. Faced with stern resistance, they were unwilling to appropriate God's provision for overcoming the foe.

Apparently Israel was not mentally prepared to meet tough, resolute opposition from their enemies. Somewhere along the line they had adopted views that were far removed from reality. Perhaps they felt that the Lord would somehow miraculously intervene, and they would not have to enter the arena to do personal combat. They were certainly remiss in failing to realize that the conquest of Canaan would be a prolonged affair that would involve their being both disciplined and tenacious. There would be no quick triumph.

It was a weakness that has afflicted saints of all ages—one that has touched most present-day believers to some degree. One of the problems, I think, springs from our eagerness to impart the joys and benefits of being a Christian to the unconverted. Thus, we tend to ignore or minimize the conflicts encountered after conversion. While it is true that salvation

8

is a free gift that is eternally received when we believe on Christ, it is also true that we can expect immediate opposition from Satan, who is dedicated to our defeat.

Our Lord made this perfectly clear when He talked to His disciples about taking up their cross and denying themselves (Lk. 9:23). Believers are to suffer no illusions; discipleship involves personal discipline, persistent opposition, and protracted development.

It is particularly important that we understand this in the early stages of our Christian lives. Satan is constantly attempting to discourage and defeat people who are in the infancy of their experience with Christ. He leaves no stone unturned in his destructive designs. Consequently, one of the great lessons we can learn from our specimen judges is that there are no easy or once-for-all triumphs this side of Heaven. Every victory won by these men was accompanied by distinct temptations to fall to some new peril. But, thankfully, God's provision for present problems is everywhere in evidence.

The seeds of Israel's failure are found in their allowing unconquered pockets of resistance to exist in their midst: "But the Jebusites dwell with the children of Benjamin in Jerusalem unto this day" (Jud. 1:21); "But the Canaanites dwelt in Gezer among them" (Jud. 1:29). They were content to coexist with their enemies and accept them as a part of their lives. It was one in a long succession of downward steps—steps that would ultimately cause a complete spiritual collapse.

A quick look at a map of the land during this period reveals three noteworthy features. First, the Israelites were virtually surrounded by their enemies. Second, in some instances they were divided from one another by concentrations of their foes. Third, the high ground, Jerusalem, was left unconquered. From this vantage point, it is easy to see that their eventual defeat was not only possible but, more likely, inevitable. In any case, under these conditions satisfactory national growth and stability were impossible.

Superimpose these considerations on our own Christian experience. What do we learn? Unconquered spiritual regions that we allow to surround us soon tend to separate us from vital communion with our Savior. These are often, particularly in our earlier experience as believers, not big things in themselves. Most of us can remember some fierce encounters with nagging habits and practices that we knew displeased God—but they were hard to shake off. The temptation was to say, *What's the harm in them? Why bother?* The same is true with so-called little things that tend to creep into our lives over the years. But, the fact is, they are divisive instruments— unconquered pockets of resistance—that tend to place our *Jerusalem* in the hands of another. We are not thoroughly yielded to His sovereign Lordship. Consequently, our fellowship with other believers becomes strained and our outreach to the lost inhibited. These things being true, our growth and joy are stymied. We stagger about wondering where the problem lies. It is no wonder that under these conditions we become frustrated, lonely, and dissatisfied.

So it was for Israel, as it is with our small transgressions: One step led to another.

They Rationalized Their Disobedience

If their adversaries were allowed to live in their midst, and if they were periodically reminded of God's command to drive them out, we can be assured that Jacob's heirs experienced occasional bouts with a troubled conscience. Theirs was a spiritually abnormal situation—one that left open only two logical conclusions: They could obey God and drive out the aliens, or they could create some palatable reason for their enemies to remain where they were. They chose the latter.

"And it came to pass, when Israel was strong, that they put the Canaanites to forced labor, and did not utterly drive them out" (Jud. 1:28).

"Neither did Zebulun drive out the inhabitants of Kitron . . . and [they] became subject to forced labor" (Jud 1:30).

"Neither did Naphtali drive out the inhabitants of Beth-shemesh . . . nevertheless, the inhabitants of Beth-shemesh and Beth-anath became subjects of forced labor" (Jud. 1:33). "But the Amorites would dwell in Mount Heres in Aijalon . . . so that they became subjects of forced labor" (Jud. 1:35).

A lack of adequate strength was not Israel's problem. Divine resources were readily available. They were, in fact, strong enough to make slaves of their foes. It follows, of course, that if they were strong enough to force these people into servitude, they were clearly able to drive them out.

The choice was made to disregard God's command and seek constructive roles for their servants to fill. They reasoned that their adversaries could carry wood and draw water, build houses and tend children. They could keep them busy enough. Their reply to Jehovah was, in effect, *Isn't this a better arrangement? We have not been so cruel as to drive them away from hearth and home. Instead, we have created legitimate reasons for them to remain in our midst.* What they were actually saying was that God's plan had been improved upon. Theirs was a better way. The fallacy of that delusion soon became apparent.

The personal applications to the situation before us are clear. The disobedient believer can never be comfortable while he is living in direct conflict with divine directives. As long as those things that are condemned in the Word and communicated through a Spirit-aroused conscience are present, we will be miserable. Our Lord says, *Put them away!* We must do so or go the way of the erring Israelites.

The overwhelming consideration is the matter of Lordship. Who, after all, is going to be the supreme commander of our lives? This is but one reason why it is vitally important to allow Him to conquer even the most insignificant habits and tendencies with which we do battle. The question always before us must be, Is this thing going to control me, or is Christ going to reign as Lord over all of my life? When we begin, after an unsuccessful struggle for victory over some habit or problem, to justify our weakness or unwillingness to see the conflict through to a God-honoring solution, we are courting spiritual disaster.

11

A friend, whom we will call Bill, offers a perfect illustration of the process. Bill was a smoker long before all of the cancer-related problems caused by tobacco were known. A hacking cough only prompted the thought that the smoker was "driving another nail in his coffin." For the sake of his friends' health and Christian testimony, Bill decided to kick the habit. For years he had suffered under the comforting delusion that he could quit any time he saw fit. After all, he reasoned, it was only a matter of willpower. However, after a few days of abstinence the reality of the situation became clear. Bill didn't have the habit; the habit had him. This was not, he discovered, child's play; it was real combat. Day in and day out the grim struggle progressed. Every whiff of smoke catching the nostril, particularly after a good meal, sent him into fitful spasms of desire. His tiny nemesis plagued him until he finally concluded that it was not worth the fight. Now the question was how to justify reinstating the smelly tormentor to its place of mastery, while at the same time creating a legitimate reason for continuing the habit.

"Well, it does give me something to do with my hands," Bill said, "and taking up gum chewing as a substitute for smoking is really bad for my teeth." This reasoning provided a glimmer of hope but admittedly was composed of pretty thin material.

"But it helps me control my weight," Bill told his protesting conscience. "After all, I'm prone to gaining excess baggage when I don't smoke. Too much weight is certainly detrimental to your health." That seemed to be it—the perfect answer. His friends and family would have to agree with this, and slim was definitely in. So the conclusion was reached that smoking would probably contribute to a more healthy state. Thus, Bill continued to foul the air and sear the eyes of his companions, all the while assuring himself that he had found the solution to his problem. Bill finally won his battle with the weed. In the process, however, he lost valuable time to become all that God intended him to be.

Another example is seen in the pastor who chafes under

the restrictions imposed by a closed study door. He finds that study can be a wearying, dreary affair. Suddenly he discovers—oddly enough, perhaps at a pastors conference—that he has been mistaken all along. Enthusiastic exhorters counsel him to forget the grinding business of balancing pastoral chores with prolonged, serious study. He learns that people can't take much expository preaching these days. It dries them up. Short sermons, punctuated by numerous stories and personal illustrations, are better suited to the climate of the times. The important thing is to get out and do something. Move! People will be impressed and helped when their pastor becomes a ubiquitous presence in the community. Especially effective is adoption of the doorbell syndrome, which keeps the preacher constantly charging about the neighborhood before dashing away to yet another "how-to" conference.

This seems very correct, necessary, and successful. That is, until the church membership begins to manifest symptoms of biblical illiteracy, spiritual anemia, and superficial ministry. Then, no amount of activity or personality power can offset the effects of neglecting the central task of the minister—that of knowledgeable, Spirit-instructed exposition of the whole counsel of God balanced by purposeful personal interaction with his people.

The term *pastor/teacher* embodies two elements: a serious, disciplined student and a caring, conscientious shepherd—in other words, a careful practitioner of balanced, ministerial life. No shortcuts.

The same case can obviously be made when we become too busy with *pressing matters* to spend time in personal meditation, prayer, and Bible study. It is a serious matter, one with which we all must come to grips.

Little problems, unattended, create big setbacks. I constantly meet Christians, in and out of what we term *full-time service*, who are unhappy, defeated people. All too often the root of their problem is found in a long string of lost *little* spiritual battles.

They Forgot The Lord

"And the children of Israel did evil in the sight of the LORD, and forgot the LORD their God" (Jud. 3:7).

Israel inevitably found that they were no longer masters over their enemies or their own fortunes. Tolerated aliens soon became welcomed bedfellows. Integration with the people and practices of the land soon took place—consorting with people who had rejected Jehovah, practicing things abhorrent to Him. Apparently, Israel had forgotten why they were to expel these people from the land. "Defile not ye yourselves in any of these things; for in all these the nations are defiled, which I cast out before you. And the land is defiled; therefore I do visit the iniquity thereof upon it, and the land itself vomiteth out her inhabitants" (Lev. 18:24-25).

Their relationship to godless people soon diverted their minds and hearts away from the great principles of faith living. They would eventually learn that God would not crown this turning from Him with His blessing. Consequently, the nation came to a state of almost complete spiritual sterility. The flesh nature had become a usurper/dictator over them.

Israel would no longer accept Jehovah's sovereignty, so it became necessary for them to find a suitable substitute for their God. Thus, the chosen people stood ready to accept satanic replacements. And now they had arrived at the last milestone of God's long-suffering before He would strike them with the rod of suffering and affliction.

Thus it was, and so it is. When we forget to give God His place, another master is put in place. Flesh begins to prevail, and Isaac Watts' lyrical question fades away in the mist of seared memories: "Is this vile world a friend to grace, to help me on to God?"

14

They Forsook the Lord

"And they forsook the LORD God of their fathers, who brought them out of the land of Egypt, and followed other gods, of the gods of the people who were round about them, and bowed themselves unto them, and provoked the LORD to anger" (Jud. 2:12).

We should pause to weep as we reflect on this poignant statement. Jehovah's pilgrim people were prostrate before the old pagan gods, locked hand in hand with the people of the land. The God who had delivered them out of the slow strangulation of Egyptian servitude was forsaken. They had descended into the pit of unbelief and disobedience until it seemed that all heavenly design and purpose for them would disappear completely. Israel was threatened by the prospect of becoming just one more heathen nation pursuing the sordid superstitions of the era. Gone were their identity, peculiarity, and spiritual prosperity. It was no longer clear that they were the people of Jehovah. The look of the world was upon them, and their actions did nothing to commend the God they had served.

How far they had fallen. They had refused to obey, rationalized their disobedience, forgotten the Lord, and forsaken their Sovereign. Israel had walked past the beckoning doorway of the privileged sanctuary to enter a squalid, heathen hovel. Their ears were deaf to His gracious word of intent: "Defile not, therefore, the land which ye shall inhabit, wherein I dwell; for I, the LORD, dwell among the children of Israel" (Num. 35:34).

It was a poor choice.

A Message at Bochim

The children of Israel may have turned away from serving the Lord, but He had not turned from them.

15

And an angel of the LORD came up from Gilgal to Bochim, and said, I made you go up out of Egypt, and have brought you unto the land which I swore to give unto your fathers; and I said, I will never break my covenant with you. And ye shall make no league with the inhabitants of this land; ye shall throw down their altars. But ye have not obeyed my voice. Why have ye done this? Wherefore I also said, I will not drive them out from before you, but they shall be as thorns in your sides, and their gods shall be a snare unto you (Jud. 2:1-3).

It was, figuratively, a long way from Gilgal to Bochim. Gilgal had been the first encampment of the fledgling nation after their passage over the Jordan. There the Lord had announced the end to which all of the miracles performed for Israel's benefit had been bent: "That all the people of the earth might know the hand of the LORD, that it is mighty, that ye might fear the LORD your God forever" (Josh. 4:24).

It was from nearby Gilgal that Joshua made his historic reconnoiter of Jericho in preparation for the first great battle in the land. It was while on this mission that he met the angel of the Lord. The heavenly emissary introduced himself as "captain of the host of the LORD" (Josh. 5:14). He told the awe-smitten son of Nun that a victory at Jericho was already in his hands. Joshua responded by falling on his face to worship in anticipation of God's impending conquest. He rose to hear the angel detail the divinely formulated battle plan.

And it came to pass, when Joshua was by Jericho, that he lifted up his eyes and looked and, behold, there stood a man over against him with his sword drawn in his hand; and Joshua went unto him, and said unto him, Art thou for us, or for our adversaries? And he said, Nay, but as captain of the host of the LORD am I now come. And Joshua fell on his face to the earth, and did worship, and said unto him, What saith my lord unto his servant? (Josh. 5:13-14).

At Bochim the angel/herald stood again before the nation's representatives, no longer garbed in heavenly armor but swathed in a garment of mourning. His present mission was not to announce an exhilarating future victory. He instead lay bare the instruments of God's chastisement. They again prostrated themselves. It was not, however, an act of worship at the prospect of promised triumph, but a wallowing in the agonies induced by their profligacy. The penalty was somberly related: "ye have not obeyed my voice . . . I will not drive them out from before you . . . they shall be as thorns in your sides . . . their gods shall be a snare unto you" (Jud. 2:2-3).

Amid these dark declarations, God raised a question, a query that they had to face corporately and individually. It was inescapable. "I said . . . ye shall make no league with the inhabitants of this land; ye shall throw down their altars. But ye have not obeyed my voice. Why have ye done this?" (Jud. 2:1-2).

"Why have ye done this?" An explanation was in order. In essence, God was asking two things: *Did you believe what I told you? Why didn't you do what you were told?* These are not, however, questions reserved for an ancient people alone. They confront each of us at this moment, and we must face them. The way in which we address them and live out our answers is the stuff of the issues we will find in this book.

Do you believe—really believe?

Will you obey?

I remember standing, head down, before my father as a boy. The occasion was the taking of an instrument from dad's sacrosanct toolbox. It had not simply been taken to be used in a small boy's urgent enterprise; it had been broken in the process. We—that is, my two brothers and I—were under the strictest of orders, articulated in the clearest possible manner: "Don't get into my toolbox." Someone obviously had. That someone happened to be me.

17

Admitting it was, in a way, the most painful part of the whole affair. But facing father, with Ken and Walter on either side, and learning that if the guilty party did not come forward we would collectively suffer the consequences, I blurted out my guilt, accompanied by profuse declarations of future good intentions. He wasn't buying it.

"Didn't I tell you not to get into my toolbox?"

"Yes, sir," I replied meekly.

"Then why did you do it?"

It was as simple as that. Try as I would to complicate the matter, the consequences for my miscreant behavior turned on what we both knew: I had heard, but I did not obey.

When we believers stand at the Bema (Judgment Seat) to receive rewards or suffer loss as our work for the Lord is evaluated, I believe that His inquiry into the conduct of our affairs as stewards and witnesses will be direct and unencumbered. I am not inclined to believe that the Judgment Seat of Christ will provide a study in the intricacies of psycho-spiritual analysis. There will, of course, be details and ramifications to face; but basically, every consideration will relate to the following elements.

Did you believe?

Did you obey?

If not, why not?

Israel could not avoid those penetrating questions, and they eventually suffered the consequences of their behavior. Their enemies were persistent sources of trouble for them, as "thorns in [their] sides" (Num. 33:55). Heathen gods deluded, distracted, and all but destroyed them. Abraham's posterity paid an extremely high price for their transgressions.

2

A Program for Victory

"Nevertheless the LORD raised up judges . . . " (Jud. 2:16).

I SRAEL WAS CREATED BY GOD for the express purpose of being a light to the nations of the earth. "I will also give thee for a light to the nations, that thou mayest be my salvation unto the end of the earth" (Isa. 49:6). Her light was not destined to flicker, fade, die, or merge with the prevailing darkness of heathenism. Consequently, "where sin abounded, grace did much more abound" (Rom. 5:20). Abounding grace for these sin-beleaguered people began to descend in two great shafts of light that broke through the night scenes of Israel's folly and failure.

The first shaft flashes out of the otherwise scathing revelation brought by the angel of the Lord as he confronted the nation at Bochim. His words were the words of God. (It may well be that this angel of the Lord was actually Jesus Christ in a preincarnate appearance.) "I made you go up out of Egypt, and have brought you unto the land which I swore to give unto your fathers; and I said, *I will never break my covenant with you*" (Jud. 2:1).

With this, the angel declared the faithfulness of God. In spite of Israel's reluctance, rebellion, and rejection, Jehovah intended to keep His word. "I will never," He affirmed, "break my covenant with you." It is a theme that was repeated often throughout the history of Jewry in like circumstances. What He promised, He would perform.

Although the heavenly visitor brought details of their coming chastisement (Jud. 2:2-3), there was no threat of national extinction. His words call to mind what the Lord had said about these people when they were in servitude to another tyrant. Moses was told, "And thou shalt say unto Pharaoh, Thus saith the LORD, Israel is my son, even my first-born" (Ex. 4:22).

As the son nation, they were sovereignly secure in Jehovah's promise. Israel would never, therefore, be dealt with like their Gentile counterparts. Their enemies would be judged; Israel would be corrected. All suffering for sin would be remedial, never a prelude to the annihilation of the nation. In this respect, Israel becomes a kind of national microcosm embodying the grand propositions that believers, Jew and Gentile, experience today as members of the body of Christ.

God had declared it; history would verify the accuracy of the pronouncement—Israel would never perish. The Old Testament, and the New for that matter, abound with prophetic texts amplifying that fact. During the nation's darkest hours, in dispersion and the throes of unparalleled trauma and decimation, God was true to His pledge of preservation. Moses made it clear as he sketched their history yet unlived: "And yet for all that, when they are in the land of their enemies, I will not cast them away, neither will I abhor them, to destroy them utterly, and to break my covenant with them; for I am the LORD their God" (Lev. 26:44).

That word shines as brightly today as it did in the Sinai and at Bochim long ago. The day of Israel's national reconciliation will come. Her Messiah will reign triumphantly over a restored nation. All of the gems of promise scattered across the pages of the Word of God will then be fulfilled. God is standing by His Word.

The magnitude of this proposition cannot be overstated. Jeremiah 31:35-37 sets forth a declaration of divine intent spelling out the limits of what man can do to the chosen people while, at the same time, declaring Jehovah's designs in the preservation of Jewry. Briefly stated, He tells us that in order to destroy Israel, it would be necessary to displace God. Only those possessing powers of omnipotence and omniscience could hope to undo what God has done in forging—before it was lived out on the stage of human history—the destiny of His people. By showing us this, the Lord presented an assuring proof text of the dimensions of the security resident in the sovereign purposes of God. What He promises, He will perform. God will not break His promises to Israel, nor will He to us!

Do you ever look at yourself as a Christian and not like what you see? I am not referring to the mirror experience which leaps to most of our minds immediately—we are all physically in a temporary state of deterioration. No, I am talking about the condition of our lives as believers. Sometimes I look at myself and deplore the pettiness, neglect, and companion detractors that I find within my being. And I wonder how, or why, God would want anything to do with me. Then words rise from the pages of the Word that captivate my mind and drive me to my knees in humility and appreciation. "And I give unto them eternal life; and they shall never perish, neither shall any man pluck them out of my hand. My Father, who gave them to me, is greater than all, and no man is able to pluck them out of my Father's hand" (Jn. 10:28-29).

My security does not, I am assured, rest in my worthiness, but in the abiding promise of His everlasting Word. Therefore, as a son, I will be corrected for disobedience. But as a *joint heir with Christ*, my relationship to Him will never be severed.

The second illuminating ray comes to us through an expressive adverb: "Nevertheless the LORD raised up judges, who delivered them out of the hand of those who spoiled them" (Jud. 2:16). Translators of the Authorized Version selected the word *nevertheless* as the vehicle through which the pivotal thought could best be conveyed. Beyond Israel's decadence and deserved chastisement lay deliverance for His people. God's *neverthelesses* would not be supplied by way of mechanisms but through *divinely chosen men*.

The process would be:

1. Brought down by their sins: "And the children of Israel did evil again in the sight of the LORD" (Jud. 3:12a).

2. Crushed beneath the weight of afflicting chastisements: "and the LORD strengthened Eglon, the king of Moab, against Israel" (Jud. 3:12b).

3. Crying out for deliverance: "But when the children of Israel cried unto the LORD" (Jud. 3:15a).

4. Rescued and restored by God-appointed men: "The LORD raised them up a deliverer" (3:15b).

The progression is repeated again and again in the Book of Judges. Just when it appeared that all was lost and the nation would be obliterated, God stepped in with a specifically chosen *nevertheless*. In an illuminating sense, the process was a prelude to the greater deliverance to be revealed in the New Testament.

As we might expect, this understanding brings even wider vistas of truth before us. It is discovered in the tiny conjunction *but*, introduced in the second chapter of Ephesians. Here the Holy Spirit exposed the sad plight of godless Gentiles: "And you hath he made alive, who were dead in trespasses and sins; In which in times past ye walked according to the course of this world, according to the prince of the power of the air, the spirit that now worketh in the sons of disobedience; Among whom also we all had our manner of life in times past in the lusts of our flesh, fulfilling the desires of the flesh and of the mind, and were by nature the children of wrath, even as others" (Eph. 2:1-3).

The brushwork of inspiration strokes a dreadful relief of our natural state. We were:

Dead in sin (Eph. 2:1).

Directed by Satan (Eph. 2:2).

Desiring fleshly gratification (Eph. 2:3).

Doomed to experience the wrath of God (Eph. 2:3b).

Just when it seems that we must resign mankind to this dismal condition and turn from any thought of a glimmer of eternal hope, we happen upon that little word *but*.

But
But God,
But God, who is rich
But God, who is rich in mercy,
But God, who is rich in mercy, for his great love
But God, who is rich in mercy, for his great love with which he loved us (Eph. 2:4).

The rivulet of revelation that found its source in the word *but* swells into a great flood tide of grace that culminates in the heart-arresting manifestation of salvation as a free gift, with converted sinners becoming the effulgence of His love and mercy.

> Even when we were dead in sins, [God] hath made us alive together with Christ (by grace ye are saved), And hath raised us up together, and made us sit together in heavenly places in Christ Jesus; That in the ages to come he might show the exceeding riches of his grace in his kindness toward us through Christ Jesus (Eph. 2:5-7).

Now we are:
Delivered from sin's penalty and power.
Deposited at Christ's side.
Displayed with Him in glory.
Destined to share His riches eternally.

But God, then, becomes the sounding bell of the gospel tolling over the heads of all among the lost who are aware of their failure and estrangement from Him. *But*—God loves; *But*—God gives; *But*—God saves; *But*—God keeps. It becomes a precious fountain of hope—hope for the hopeless; help for the helpless.

Born estranged, in condemnation,
Heir apparent of damnation.
Taken prey in fetters strong;
Naturally inclined to wrong.

But God falls on craven ear,
Grace and *mercy*, too, I hear.
Fall to own capitulation;
Rise resplendent in salvation.

Nevertheless

While the Ephesians passage sings of heavenly help for the sinner, Judges orchestrates over the lives of beleaguered believers—those wearied by their insignificance and others who for years have cowered before fears and finally resigned commissions as heralds of the gospel in favor of a life lived out under the circumstances. It speaks afresh to saints who feel isolated because of a bad start in life. Finally, it brings soothing balm to those who have failed the Lord since becoming Christians—that one who has had every spiritual advantage, only to bring disgrace to his Lord, church, and personal profession.

Each of these, in his or her own situation, has been manipulated by Satan into a position of preoccupation with failures or deficiencies. They are fully convinced that they are, after all, different from other believers. Theirs, they come to believe, is a special case with peculiar problems. It is, therefore, impossible for them to live lives aglow with the radiance of Christ. This delusion is one of the most subtle and successful traps sprung on the unwary among us.

If you are inclined to live among the aforementioned, there is wonderful news. For every disheartened child of light, God has a personal *nevertheless*. "And when the LORD raised them up judges, then the LORD was with the judge, and delivered them out of the hand of their enemies all the days of the judge; for it repented the LORD because of their groanings by reason of them who oppressed them and vexed them" (Jud. 2:18).

These Four Men

"And what shall I more say? For the time would fail me to tell of Gideon, and of Barak, and of Samson, and of Jephthah" (Heb. 11:32).

27

Four men were selected from the period of the judges to be included among the heroes of the faith. Others were passed over, while these were chosen. Why was this so?

First, it is important to reemphasize that our Lord never does anything capriciously. There is always a clear purpose, one designed for our blessing and benefit. These men were awarded the privilege of coming before us because each had features in his life's makeup, which, when exposed, could be used by the Holy Spirit to aid saints in all future generations. It is, therefore, essential that we look at these men, not simply with idle curiosity, but with receptive hearts and minds.

To accomplish this, there are three general areas we must address. This can best be done by asking some simple questions:

1. What were the circumstances in which these men found themselves?

2. What kind of men were they?

3. What were the common characteristics shared by Barak, Gideon, Jephthah, and Samson?

First, the circumstances.

We begin with an obvious but often overlooked fact. This was a time in history when not one of the major empires was on the prowl against Israel. Proud Nebuchadnezzar and his Babylonian hordes had not yet hammered the known world into submission. The Golden Greek, Alexander, with his flying Macedonians, was standing in the wings off the stage of another era. The imperial majesty of the Caesars and their legions was also unknown.

Each of these predator nations conjures up a certain sense of awesome dignity. They were world empires, and history bears a large mark from each of them. But how much space is given in the historical journals to the Philistines, Midianites, or, indeed, the Canaanites? The best way in which we dignify their memory is to list them among the pestiferous *gnat* nations of antiquity. They had petty kings with equally petty ambitions. These nations would have drawn scant attention except for the startling impact they made on God's chosen people. Abraham's seed fell before them with astonishing regularity, until they finally reached one of the lowest plateaus recorded in the spiritual history of Israel—the days of the judges. The lesson is evident, but we must linger to comprehend its application. Confronted by a Rome, Greece, or Babylon, they knew soon enough what to do. In their impotence, they looked and longed for divine solutions. In all of these periods they held fondly to the messianic hope, which promised to bring deity upon the scene to soundly thrash and depose their oppressors. However, as we have already learned, for long years they felt that they were quite competent to handle these *little* problems. It was only after the consequences had decimated the nation that they belatedly sought divine assistance.

In our own lives, we are seldom confronted by imperial-size problems. When we are, most of us are well prepared as to the proper course of action to pursue. The immensity of great crisis situations dwarfs our ability to respond adequately. We therefore quickly prostrate ourselves before God to seek out His solution. But, really, most of our problems are more like terrier-sized, Midianite-type confrontations. It is with such problems that we frequently experience failure.

The late Dr. James McGinlay told the story of an experience he had while preaching in the Canadian wilderness. One snowy afternoon he decided to engage a sleigh for a jaunt through the woods. At a particularly picturesque spot in the road, he stopped the sleigh and ventured forth on foot. Suddenly, while walking around a large tree, he found himself face-to-face with an enormous bear. Needless to say, he beat a hasty and somewhat unceremonious retreat.

Dr. McGinlay contrasted this experience with another encounter he had had at a summer conference in Florida. A short time after retiring one night, he heard the incessant whine of a flying mosquito piercing the silence. He popped out of bed to do battle with his tiny tormentor. But when the light went on, the adversary was nowhere to be found. Throughout the night, the grim little disquieter eluded Dr. McGinlay's most determined efforts to destroy his foe. The next morning the revered lecturer went on his way, frayed and testy.

He concluded that there was a sort of dignity born of crisis in the bear-sized problem. But it was the mosquito that inflicted the most devastating wounds.

How true! And what a familiar ring that tale has for us. This is where we live. It is the great battleground of life. It is here that we rise or fall as overcomers—in the day-to-day, while the rounds of repetitious responsibilities grind away at us. We keep waiting for something big to happen to us. It seldom does. But then, after all, why should Satan use cannons, when small darts can more effectively accomplish his purposes?

We can conclude that our prayerlessness, neglect of personal communion with God, unwieldy tempers, proneness to procrastinate, and the like most often cause us to become the bedfellows of defeat. Our attention must be fixed on being victorious in these areas, if we ever expect to be prepared to face the larger issues of the Christian life.

A Lesson from the Silent Years

Few of us have taken time to meditate upon those silent years of purposeful obscurity in the life of our Lord before He began His public ministry. We pass over them because of the lack of specific information available to us. There is, however, an element apparent in those years that we can ill afford to miss.

We readily and appreciatively view the monumental victories won by Christ. Demons cowered before Him. Satan was met and mastered. One by one, the great enemies of our souls were led to Him, there to be humiliated and divested of their mastery. And, at last, a banner of victory was waved across the mouth of an empty tomb. He is a triumphant Savior.

But remember this: He was the God-Man for the whole of His life—just as much during those silent years as in the time of public exposure. While the lack of specific information cautions against undue speculation, we can learn a fundamental truth by a few moments of careful reflection on this period.

Jesus spent these years in Nazareth, an isolated hamlet

familiar to all of us. It was isolated in the sense of being removed from the center of Jewish religious life. But the isolation was both geographical and ideological. The Galileans were purposely excluded from the theological mainstream of Judaism. The area was caustically referred to as "Galilee of the Gentiles." Nathanael voiced a like sentiment when he questioned any good thing coming out of Nazareth. The point is, Jesus Christ did not receive His early training in company with theologians. He received it in a carpenter's shop.

This was a well-calculated move on the part of the Father. Remember, our Lord was fully divine, yet He was also fully human—thus the designation, the God-Man. It was the perfect fusion of deity and humanity. While this concept admittedly beggars our powers of comprehension, we must acknowledge that, in His humanity, Christ experienced life as it has been with every individual ever born on this earth. He was sinless, to be sure, but was touched with the feeling of our infirmities: "For we have not an high priest who cannot be touched with the feeling of our infirmities, but was in all points tempted like as we are, yet without sin" (Heb. 4:15).

What was He doing during those quiet years?

As the sun brushed the snows of Mount Hermon, on its way to spread pink fingers over Galilee, He would have long since been up and about. He could be found in Joseph's simple tradesman's shop, working with tools that were less than perfect. Jesus must have known the problems involved in dealing with people who were hard to satisfy. He was often, no doubt, found on a scaffold at some local dwelling under construction. He worked under the sweltering summer sun and in winter's chill. Perhaps Jesus was called upon to enter a stable and fit a new yoke to the neck of some local farmer's recalcitrant ox.

At home, He companioned with mother and father, brothers and sisters, who were just as human as yours and mine. The sometimes tedious and taxing round of household affairs and the sheer weariness of dragging, repetitious duties were all a part of His life, too.

The Sabbath found Him in the local synagogue lifting a hearty voice of praise with the men of the city. He read the Book, retired for prayer, brought His tithe, endured the hypocrites, and chafed under the inconsistencies and superficialities of some of His fellows. During the great national festivals He was amid the throngs pressing the road up to Jerusalem. The nights spent along the way were passed in facilities that were often less than pleasant, with some people who were also abrasive.

Our blessed Lord emerged from those years absolutely victorious. He was without blemish—unsullied by the wiles of the day-to-day routine. In other words, Jesus Christ triumphed over the mundane! The Scriptures lay great weight on this fact, and then offer His resources to us—heavenly provision for the meanest occupations of this life.

In considering all that lies before us, let us remember that it is in the strength of His victory that we will find our own.

Next, what kind of men were these deliverers?

They were just like we are! It can be readily asserted, and firmly so, that they were men of *like passions*. This is, of course, another of those statements easier declared than assimilated. How prone we all are to relegate Bible characters to the *great saint* category. In so doing, we sever the practical implications of their experiences from any relevant relationship to our own. We must resolutely guard against this. If we are to be properly instructed and profit from our study of the lives before us, we must stop placing them in an untouchable caste and, instead, see them brought down to our own level of life and potential. The truth is, we have available to us every resource necessary to place us in precisely the same position attained by these worthies in their supreme acts of heroism—every resource and more.

I recall a vivid illustration of this from my early days in the ministry. In the congregation of the rural church I served was a lady who had been a shut-in for years. She suffered the ravages of rheumatoid arthritis and was held captive in a body that was drawn and in constant pain. Her arms bore numerous scars from burns inflicted while she tended the cooking with a relentless determination not to relinquish her household responsibilities. Her vision was impaired to the point that she could read only with great difficulty, aided by two pairs of glasses, one tilted precariously over the other. She wore a hearing aid, a rather comical contraption of ancient vintage. Occasionally, for no apparent reason, it would emit high-pitched screeches—to the extreme discomfort of all within earshot.

On visits she would most often be found seated before her kitchen window, laboriously reading a huge large-print Bible. Spending some time with this diminutive saint was somewhat akin to conversing with spiritual royalty. Her perpetual smile, her quick wit, and the total disdain with which she dismissed her infirmities, coupled with a rare eagerness to plunge into the mainstream of the Word, made one immediately aware of being in the company of a most uncommon individual.

One day, as I was entering her little kitchen-sanctuary, she called triumphantly, "Would you like to know why I am like I am?"

"Why certainly, if you can tell me," I replied.

Her gnarled fingers swept through the pages of that old Bible like a skipping school girl. When she had found the place, she began to read: "Thou hast dealt well with thy servant, O LORD, according unto thy word . . . Before I was afflicted I went astray, but now have I kept thy word . . . It is good for me that I have been afflicted, that I might learn thy statutes" (Ps. 119:65, 67, 71).

She peered over her glasses and with an intent seriousness explained that if she had not experienced physical suffering, she probably would not have known Christ. She was certain, she added, that she would not have known the Bible as she did. She viewed all that she had been forced to endure, compared it with what she had gained from her enforced seclusion, and declared emphatically that she had gained far more, and for eternity, than she had given up to her infirmity.

Mrs. Nance had met her personal Canaanite, Midianite, and

Philistine and, through appropriating God's promises, put them to flight. I can say, without the slightest hesitation, that a frail arthritic who has learned the principles of faith living and Bible obedience is on equal footing with those we rightly revere as heroes of the faith. There is not one iota of difference between them. When one's spiritual foes are met and conquered, the believer joins the ranks of those illustrious Bible champions.

All of this, then, opens glowing avenues of possibility to us. Our names can be placed alongside the *Gideons, Davids,* and *Pauls* of the Scripture. This is not fantasizing; it is fact. It is indeed a fact that is basic to our becoming what He would have us to be. God has adequate resources available to us; we must learn to use the keys that will appropriate them.

Finally, what were the basic characteristics shared by these four men?

They are twofold, direct and simple—*faith* and *obedience.* Although there were vast differences in their personalities and problems, these men shared a common ability to believe the Word of God and then obey it.

We Christians are, all too often, afflicted with an attitude that surfaced in a statement made by a man I had led to Christ. He had patiently listened to the plan of salvation. After I had explained it, he eagerly accepted Christ as his personal Savior. Then I asked, "Now, James, are you sure that you are a child of God?"

"Yes, I am," he replied emotionally. "This is what I have been searching for all of my life. But I see now, I've been trying to make it more difficult that God did."

This is not only a problem with the lost. It is very much a problem with the believer's attitude about this business of Christian living. We read multiplied volumes that promote formulas for spiritual achievement. Our minds are set awhirl by some of the nearly mystical vaporisms of books with titles like *Seven Secret Steps to Spiritual Success,* which promote the idea that Christian victory is gained by employing some recently discovered system that is complex and awash with hyperspiritual jargon, catchwords, and mathematical pyramids. This may all be well and good for the initiated, but the rest of us do well to remind ourselves that Christianity is for ordinary human beings, too. A great deal is made of the fact that salvation is simple enough for a child to understand. If this is true—and it demonstrably is—then why insist on making Christian living something that amounts to spiritual calculus? The longer one lives, the more evident it becomes that all of us are made of very ordinary stuff. Some of us may, indeed, prove to be more *ordinary* than others. But each of us, with our individual spiritual gifts and God-given intellectual capacity, can find His will and be exactly what He wants us to be. Although there are, admittedly, manifold ramifications in every area of development in the Christian life, the basic propositions are arrow straight and crystal clear—*believe God; obey God.*

This program for victory is wonderfully demonstrated in the lives of God's four ordinary men.

3

BARAK—The Faceless

BARAK—THE FACELESS

Comes Jabin like a foul plague
　To smite the chosen seed,
And with him noxious Sisera
　To consummate the deed.

Great chariots of iron roll,
　Nine hundred by the count,
To turn Esdraelon's comely plain
　Into a bloody fount.

Far up on Tabor's wooded slope
　Waits Barak and his host.
A man quite ill equipped, it seems,
　To stand a warrior's post.

But this man holds the surest sword
　God's foes to recompense.
The tempered, twin-edged,
　Heaven-forged blades—
　　FAITH and OBEDIENCE.

And the children of Israel again did evil in the sight of the LORD, when Ehud was dead. And the LORD sold them into the hand of Jabin, king of Canaan, who reigned in Hazor, the captain of whose host was Sisera, who dwelt in Harosheth of the nations. And the children of Israel cried unto the LORD; for he had nine hundred chariots of iron; and twenty years he mightily oppressed the children of Israel. And Deborah, a prophetess, the wife of Lapidoth, judged Israel at that time. And she dwelt under the palm tree of Deborah, between Ramah and Bethel in Mount Ephraim; and the children of Israel came up to her for judgment. And she sent and called Barak, the son of Abinoam, out of Kedesh-naphtali, and said unto him, Hath not the LORD God of Israel commanded, saying, Go and draw toward Mount Tabor, and take with thee ten thousand men of the children of Naphtali and of the children of Zebulun? And I will draw unto thee, to the river Kishon, Sisera, the captain of Jabin's army, with his chariots and his multitude; and I will deliver him into thine hand. And Barak said unto her, If thou wilt go with me, then I will go; but if thou wilt not go with me, then I will not go. And she said, I will surely go with thee: notwithstanding, the journey that thou takest shall not be for thine honor; for the LORD shall sell Sisera into the hand of a woman. And Deborah arose, and went with Barak to Kedesh (Jud. 4:1-9).

I SRAEL'S FAILURE TO BELIEVE and obey God created a slowly festering sore on the anatomy of the nation. They would ultimately fall beneath the weight of a canker that they had allowed to become far too large and painful to excise with their own hands. The inhabitants of the land, whose presence among them seemed inconsequential at the beginning, soon produced Jabin, Sisera, and nine hundred chariots of iron. Consequently, the children of Israel found themselves terrorized, oppressed, and faced with 20 years of debilitating servitude.

The Canaanites

As the Israelites labored under the oppression of Jabin and Sisera, the beautiful hills in the central and northern part of the country must have taken on a harsh and foreboding appearance. Those 20 years seemed to pass at a snail's pace as the children of Israel were *mightily oppressed* by the Canaanite king.

The Canaanites far surpassed all of their contemporaries in lust, cruelty, and degrading spiritual practices. Their religion consisted of adoration of the planets and worship of a pantheon of gods, El being the supreme deity. Baal was the chief underling of El and overlord of the lesser gods in the pantheon. Baal was identified as the *god of rain and the storm*, whose voice rode the heavens on wings of the thunderclaps. His images depicted him holding a thunderbolt shaped into a spear. Their circle of gods also contained female figures. Astarte, Asherah, and Anath were believed to possess the power to change their gender as the occasion dictated.

Without spelling out sensual details, it must be noted that this grouping of gods and goddesses promoted the most detestable sexual excesses. Promiscuity, incest, and nudity were all glorified among the gods of Canaan. Sacred prostitution and sodomy were also prominent in the licentious practices of these false deities. Canaanite worship can only be characterized as a gross perversion of everything sacred to true people of God.

We must remember that these gods were created by the people who embraced them. And, if it can be said that religion influences moral conduct, it is equally true that the gods men create are only, in the final analysis, a reflection of the human debauchery of those who form them.

Canaanites were also known for their love of brutality. Sisera's nine hundred chariots of iron were one obvious evidence of this fact. In one ancient account of the history of these people and their gods, Anath is seen in an orgy of death and destruction, wading through human blood up to her knees while slaughtering innocent children and adults. With this picture in mind, one may well understand why the Canaanite oppression was such an agonizing experience for the chosen people.

For Israel, with her unique mission among the nations of the world, any attempt to coexist with such a people was unthinkable. Their association with the morals and worship of the Canaanites could only result in spiritual catastrophe. The nation was on her way to fulfilling the lofty purposes to which God had called her—and the path was designed to be consistently onward and upward. To consort with a nation that had hit rock bottom spiritually and was only a short step removed from destruction was simply intolerable.

One can, therefore, easily understand why God commanded Israel to drive out the Canaanites—an act frequently condemned by liberal religionists. In reality, it was an act of mercy. God was attempting to spare Israel the agonies she would, unfortunately, choose to suffer.

The Book of Judges repeatedly confronts us with the depressing regularity of Israel's descent into the quagmire of sin-saturated disobedience. Dismal choices were consistently made by the nation and its leaders to taste the fruits of the flesh, which were totally abhorrent to God. *Sin*, indeed, *abounded* among the chosen people.

Yes, God would faithfully apply His abounding *grace* and rescue them from the treacherous pit they had dug for themselves. But inevitably there were residual problems and irretrievably lost ground that would cloud their future.

We do well to remember that all of Israel's deliverers only lifted the nation back to the level on which Jehovah wanted them to live all along. While He was faithful in bringing them out of their sinful spirals, these episodes were dreadfully costly affairs. They were encounters for which the joy of recovery was little compensation for the wasted years of suffering. When it was all over, the bitter memories and scars of their defection were etched on the national countenance. Beyond this were the resident temptations resulting from their sinning that would beset the people again and again during times of spiritual low ebb.

When we apply these facts to our present easy attitude toward sin and its consequences, we soon recognize the need for an immediate shift in our thinking. Many of the current movements, which take an almost flippant attitude toward conduct frowned upon in Scripture, are doing modern Christians a grave disservice. Catchphrases that promise effortlessly to restore the errant believer to a place of blessing are a delusion. Sin in any form is an offense to God. To call this to the attention of believers is not to engage in sanctimonious legalism. It is a warning that must be sounded. We must develop a sensitivity to sin and acquire a new appreciation of the need for true holiness in life.

Send Us A Man

"And the children of Israel cried unto the LORD" (Jud. 4:3). The people finally came to the end of themselves and realized that there was no hope apart from divine deliverance. God would have to send them a man who could drive out their enemies. In the cold light of the circumstances, he must prove to be a man with audacious courage—one who could confront the foe on the one hand, while withstanding the weaknesses of his own people on the other. Above all else, he must be a man singularly chosen and obviously equipped for the task by God.

What kind of man did God choose?

As Israel lifted an agonizing lament, the Lord made His selection, and Barak, the son of Abinoam, silently slipped from the wings. On the surface, for reasons that we shall pursue, he would seem the least likely of all the judges to be entered in the *Hall of Heroes*. His most noteworthy attribute to this point was his obscurity. All that is said, by way of introduction, is that he hailed from Kedesh-naphtali, an old city of refuge near the Sea of Galilee.

Barak therefore stands as the symbol of the *faceless man*. He is that individual who seems, at first glance, to be just another face in the crowd—an unknown, passed over by the masses, yet one possessing those sterling qualities so indispensable to the work of God. It may be significant that inspiration has singled him out to occupy the first position among the four judges selected for study. It may be that our Lord would have us pay tribute to a man who is the prototype *follower*, one who was there when the crisis came, who stepped from obscurity to lead God's people to a magnificent victory, and who then returned to his quiet place, never to be heard from again.

Discerning Deborah

"And Deborah, a prophetess, the wife of Lapidoth, judged Israel at that time" (Jud. 4:4).

The mantle of leadership rested upon the shoulders of a stalwart woman at this time. It seemed an unusual arrangement for a nation facing unusual problems. But she was there, divinely placed, charged with the responsibility of choosing the man with the best qualifications to lead Israel against the foe.

This woman was a steely-eyed, no-nonsense type of person, and I, for one, wonder just how comfortable it would be for most males to serve under Judge Deborah. My impression is that when she told people to step, they stepped. In other words, she was a woman with a character tempered to face chariots of iron.

But this was not, in my opinion, her greatest attribute. There were, no doubt, many Jewish *Don Quixotes* available who were quite willing to *run where the brave dare not go*. But foolhardy adventurers were not the champions who would win the day for Israel and God. No, it must be a special person for a very special job, and Deborah had the God-given discernment to pick the right man. This was her real strength as a leader— making the right choice and then standing with him until the victory was won.

As we shall observe, Deborah saw in Barak a quality that he obviously did not recognize in himself. He was hesitant when it came to assessing his own ability to handle the task at hand, but she never wavered in her belief that he was the man God had chosen.

This is a magnificent quality. And we must at every opportunity press the need to exercise today the kind of discernment Deborah displayed. Blessed is the church with a number of encouraging discerners in their midst—those who see through people's problems to their potential for God.

I know a pastor, now with the Lord, who had an ability to see ministering gifts in some outwardly questionable prospects for Christian work. But through discerning, discipling, encouraging, and providing opportunities for service, that man was God's instrument in placing a host of men in the ministry and on the mission field. All of us know people like him, and most of us have been affected by someone like him along the way. The lesson here, I think, is for each of us to ask the Lord for a sensitive spirit and an eye for qualities in people, young and old, which can emerge for blessing and service.

Barak was a man who, quite literally, did not know his own strength. His foundational problem was a lack of *recognition* of his own worth and ability. Consequently he was devoid of the kind of confidence necessary to face adversaries, battle, and bloodshed. This weakness surfaced in his statement to Deborah.

God's message to Barak, through Deborah, was to muster ten thousand men and take them to Mount Tabor. "And I will draw unto thee, to the river Kishon, Sisera, the captain of Jabin's army, with his chariots and his multitude; and I will deliver him into thine hand" (Jud. 4:7). Barak's response was, "If thou [Deborah] wilt go with me, then I will go; but if thou wilt not go with me, then I will not go" (Jud. 4:8). Israel's select son laid down a condition. He would go out to battle only if Deborah went with him to the site of the conflict. If she refused, he too would demur.

Barak apparently had a confidence crisis. He evidently felt that he was not cut from the same cloth as others who had led Israel in bygone days. This is a common difficulty. We set certain patterns in our minds about the types of people we believe are capable of performing deeds of great spiritual magnitude. What we fail to see is the uniqueness of each individual believer and the fact that it is God who enables us to perform any task to which we are called. The fact that we are unknown is of no consequence whatever to God. We are known by Him! And that is what makes us worthy champions of His purposes. How often Satan intimidates Christians by pressing the thought that we are, after all, really nobodies. The cause of Christ, he counsels, can get on very well without our playing an obvious role. In Barak's case, it could be argued, Deborah was already on the scene. No one questioned her ability to lead. Why should a nobody like Barak clutter up the landscape? And so it goes. Often under this kind of pressure, we withdraw into a shell of insignificance, never appreciating or employing those gifts and talents that God has vested in us. In so doing, we are guilty of denying God the opportunity to use us as He wills. We may call it humility; God calls it disobedience.

If you think you are being called upon to face responsibilities that seem beyond your capacities, consider Barak. In addition to his apparent lack of confidence, he was confronted by factors that tended to confirm, rather than allay, his fears. He was called upon to face the equivalent of a huge armored force with only an ill-equipped army of foot soldiers. He was to be responsible for marshaling the army that would follow him in this seemingly impossible quest. Other seeds of discouragement are found in five additional considerations.

1. There is no record that he ever received direct personal communication from Jehovah. This was often the case with other judges, but never with Barak.

2. He was never confronted by a messenger from God. This happened to Gideon in a dramatic encounter at the threshing floor. Barak was not singled out for such spectacular episodes.

3. There is no reference to the Spirit of the Lord coming upon him. This is repeatedly stated of other judges, but not of Barak.

4. Every word of instruction he received from God came through a female agent. Deborah was the transmitter of the divine plan to the commanding general of the forces of Israel.

5. He was specifically informed that he would receive no honor for the victory, but that any accolades to be garnered would fall to a woman, not to him: "And she said, I will surely go with thee: notwithstanding, the journey that thou takest shall not be for thine honor; for the LORD shall sell Sisera into the hand of a woman" (Jud. 4:9).

One need not accuse any hesitant male of having chauvinist tendencies under these circumstances. This was no light thing that Barak was asked to do. He was called upon to be a

Committed,

Confident,

Courageous,

Condescending

Conqueror.

And all of this was on the word of a woman. Would his decision make him famous or foolhardy?

There can be little question about it, Barak faced some distinct problems as he undertook the leadership of the army of ancient Israel.

The Consummate Follower

Barak's fundamental qualities are illuminated by the problems he encountered. Such a formidable array of potential barriers seem to demand some rather complicated solutions. This was not the case, however, because Barak was a believer! He accepted the Word of God as it came to him through Deborah. He did not need it to come in a flash of fire or through an angelic medium. It was the Word of God, and the Word of God was to be accepted and acted upon. This is what must have caught the eye of Deborah. Here was a man who could believe God. He could believe God in the face of overwhelming human obstacles. He could believe God in spite of his low estimate of himself. The son of Abinoam apparently had a quiet and abiding confidence in the strength of the Word of the Lord.

Joined to his ability to believe was a simple determination to obey God, just to do those things he was convinced were of God. This is where many of us suffer spiritual breakdowns. We learn what to do but fail in the doing. Barak accepted Deborah's communication as marching orders from Jehovah.

Rudyard Kipling, in his *Charge of the Light Brigade*, said of his storied six hundred, "Theirs not to make reply, Theirs not

49

to reason why, Theirs but to do and die." This kind of obedience is expressive of the set-jawed character of Barak. Kipling's soldiers were, of course, flinging themselves forward in an act of regimental futility. Barak, however, had a superior Commander, one who had formulated a battle plan that he could accept without question or hesitation. God's man could not see all of the landscape of victory at the moment, but he could march forward in the assurance of promised victory.

Obedience is ever the watchword for Christian confidence and fulfillment. Life's greatest satisfaction is found in following God's orders to the best of our ability, simply doing what we are told to do.

Blessed, indeed, is the pastor who can look over his congregation and see a host of *Baraks*. The supreme manifestation of quality Christianity is to be seen in the lives of those noble individuals who have learned to be disciplined and dedicated followers, those who have the capacity to believe and obey. We spend much of our time talking and writing about *great* preachers and the *great* churches they have built. But there would be no great preachers or great churches without many, many *great followers!* We ministers tend, at times, to take them for granted, but how utterly helpless we would be without them.

Jim had some formidable disadvantages. He lost his mother when he was just a lad. She was a Christian who stood by him as the only source of light in a rather dismal world. Following her death, he was not sent to school, so he never learned to read or write. Ungodliness was the rule of thumb for the environment in which he found himself. Jim, however, could never shake off the memory of his mother's life of love for Christ or the thought of kneeling beside her as she prayed for her boy.

Those cherished memories drove him to Christ, and when Jim came to the Lord, he brought with him all that he possessed and laid it at the feet of his Savior. From the outset, he was a supreme example of a committed follower. Although he couldn't read himself, he asked his pastor to mark salvation verses in his Bible so that he could patiently show people from the Scripture how to come to Christ. Ever thereafter, Jim was a man you could count on. Saints and sinners alike found in him a steadfast servant of man and God. He was faithful to every phase of the work of his church and a constant encouragement to pastors, Christian workers, and trudging fellow believers.

When he went home to be with the Lord, the crowd that overflowed the church sanctuary heard a long-time friend and preacher of the gospel say, "If I were asked to name one man who was more like Christ than anyone else I have known, it would be Jim." In Jim he had met a man who had learned to follow, and it was the follower who showed many the way to Christ.

Roll Kishon, Roll

It was hard by the banks of the Kishon that Barak was to find the divine answer to his problems of recognition and lack of self-confidence. "And I will draw unto thee, to the river Kishon, Sisera, the captain of Jabin's army, with his chariots and his multitude; and I will deliver him into thine hand" (Jud. 4:7).

Jabin and Sisera were delighted to hear that Barak and ten thousand Hebrew foot soldiers had gathered on the slopes of Mount Tabor. They would engage him on the Plain of Esdraelon, a place perfectly suited to the use of their chariots. A great host of infantry was at Sisera's disposal for the work of mopping up after the onslaught of the chariots. The Canaanites' passion for cruelty must have risen to fever pitch at the prospect of a great and bloody triumph over lowly Israel. It was not to be, however; God had other plans. Before the veil of evening fell over the events of the day, Israel would win an astonishing victory, and Barak would know his true worth to Jehovah.

As Barak and his men crouched apprehensively on the sides of the mountain, the skies began to darken. They paid scant

51

attention to this, for stretched out before them in the valley below was an awe-inspiring spectacle: The armies of Jabin had assembled for the task at hand. Menacing chariots were drawn up behind long rows of splendid horses. Assembled contingents of troops, with their flowing banners and glistening spears, were an impressive sight, to say the least. Nor would these waiting warriors take much note of the sprinkle beginning to wet their backs as they peered intently through the trees in an effort to single out the form of the celebrated Sisera. The rain eventually commanded their attention, however, for it soon swept the plain with bone-chilling intensity. We can almost hear one of Barak's disgruntled privates, in true military fashion, exclaim, *It's not bad enough that we've come out here to die; now we must do it cold and wet!* But, as is so often the case, what seemed a severe trial was turned into a stunning triumph.

Even as Barak's band quit the woods to enter the plain and initiate the battle, the verdant valley was turned into a quagmire. The animals were terror-stricken as great flashes of lightning, accompanied by deafening claps of thunder, split the heavens. The rain became so intense that the Kishon, normally little more than a dry wash, leaped its banks and rolled out across Esdraelon. Plunging horses and mired chariots soon made it evident to Sisera that there was but one logical course of action open to him—to make a run for it. His army began to retreat in total disarray and thus became easy prey for the sons of Abraham, who resolutely pursued them to Harosheth-hagoyim. "And all the host of Sisera fell upon the edge of the sword; and there was not a man left" (Jud. 4:16).

The follower became the pursuer; the pursuer became the victor; the victory was the Lord's.

Two things happened that day: First, *God identified with Barak.* How could he feel insignificant or intimidated when God so obviously identified with His man in the arena of combat? In the place of true testing, Jehovah demonstrated, once and for all, that Barak was a man who stood second to none in the divine scheme of things.

Many believers never don this garland of victory because they refuse to enter the arena where God can prove His power and properly recognize His man or woman. We are so self-intimidated that we simply refuse to try. How many of us have never come to a place of useful service because we seem to be preprogrammed to refuse all opportunities that come our way? We do not allow God to prove Himself to us or exhibit His power through us. But it shouldn't be this way, nor need it be, if we, like Barak, will step out and try.

I once closed a missions conference with a challenge to the congregation to commit themselves to attempting something they had never before done for the Lord. The church bulletin that week contained a variety of opportunities for service in the church.

"Take a sheet of paper," I said. "Write down just one thing you will try—at least try—to accomplish for the Lord."

After the service, the associate pastor came to me. "Elwood," he exclaimed, "the most wonderful thing just happened. My son-in-law, who has not been a Christian for very long, came to show me what he had written on his sheet of paper." "I'll patrol the parking lot for Jesus," the son-in-law had penned triumphantly. Among the options I had mentioned to the congregation was the need for volunteers to patrol the church grounds on Halloween in order to guard against vandalism. "I can't teach a class yet," the young fellow went on, "but I can patrol the parking lot."

I haven't followed his development since, but if that young man continued with his *I'll try* spirit, he is somewhere faithfully and effectively serving the Lord.

Second, *God proved that the battle was, after all, His, and He accomplished the victory.* In ancient days, battles were not simply fought army against army, or even nation against nation. It was also god against god, or, as in this case, God against gods. The Canaanites had defied Jehovah; He would not abide their arrogance. When the battle was joined, the result was unmistakable—both battle and glory were His.

The Canaanite god Baal was *the god of the storm.* They claimed

53

that he ruled supreme over the elements. God chose a means that fully exposed the folly of this delusion.

Jehovah Himself mounted the wings of the wind and rode above the storm. With the lightning shaft as His spear and the raindrop as His missile, He reduced His belligerent adversaries to humiliated object lessons of history. Baal, in whom they had trusted, was but an impotent figment of the imaginations of the men who had created him. The Lord God of Israel controlled the heavens and ruled over the affairs of men and nations.

Interestingly, He repeated the process when Elijah contested with the prophets of Baal at a later time. On that occasion rain was withheld by Jehovah from those who worshiped the god who, they supposed, controlled the rain. As Elijah stood before his altar on Carmel, surrounded by priestly emissaries of Baal, a lightning bolt from heaven devoured the sacrifice and identified God's prophet for king and peasant alike. In these acts, God broke the hold of the satanic tyrants and put to rest any speculation about His person and power.

Christians must be aware of the principles for living exhibited in these victories. Any shaft of satanic opposition or temptation is actually fashioned to strike through us and beyond to afflict God. This is Satan's real motivation. Therefore, whenever we are engaged in heated combat with our old enemy, his quarrel is actually with our Lord. It follows, then, that our best weapons are to be found in complete dependence on God. Rather than developing elaborate schemes for self-protection and offensive combat, we are to retreat quickly into His provision and allow Him to equip us for the victory.

Ephesians 6:10-18 identifies the implements of our spiritual preparation. In verse 11 we are *admonished* to "Put on the whole *armor of God*." Thus, we are charged to be obedient in the matter of appropriating what He supplies. In other words, obedience demands diligence in preparing ourselves to stand effectively for Him.

Our *adversaries* are identified in verse 12. From top to bottom, in the spheres that are now temporarily under the dominion of Satan, the "prince of the power of the air" (Eph. 2:2), we are confronted by an array of evil forces commensurate with the fabled *chariots of iron* faced by our spiritual forebear Barak. Recognizing the impotence of every fleshly resource against such *powers of darkness* motivates us quickly to put on the *armor of God*.

Verses 14-17 define the *armor* against which every vulnerable area of the believer's being is successfully shielded from attack by the adversary. The Word of God, truth, righteousness, the gospel of peace, faith, and salvation combine to equip us for defensive and offensive spiritual warfare. The emphasis on appropriation by faith—"Above all . . . the shield of faith" (v. 16)—once again places before us the indispensable propositions: Obey God (v. 11) and believe God (v. 16).

Finally, verse 18 commends perfect *assurance* as we watch and pray in the power of the enabling Spirit of God. Such is the rest He supplies in the face of the worst this world can hurl at us.

The Outgrowth Problem

Barak had won a resounding victory; the people were delivered; the land came to rest. Satan, however, was not through with our specimen judge. He was to learn what each of us must: There is never *final* victory this side of Heaven. This may shock some, because we are now beyond the point at which most accounts of spiritual trial and triumphs are closed. Barak came through the crisis to victory and blessing and, after the time-honored pattern, should have *lived happily ever after*. Nothing could be further from reality. As a matter of fact, it is often while we are standing on the pinnacle of some great spiritual victory, experiencing the full flood of emotion accompanying such occasions, that Satan launches some swift assault that brings us from the summit to the valley in short order. Indeed, the problem may be a direct outgrowth of the victory we have enjoyed.

If this seems strange, we need but examine the full accounts of the experiences of our four judges. Each encountered a definite problem as a consequence of his victory. Of course, one will immediately acknowledge that if this is true, we must be prepared to be vigilant and dependent on the Lord continually and not just sporadically. This is precisely what God is trying to get through to us. We resist accepting the fact that in this life we will always have to deal with struggles and trials in one form or another. As a result, we gravitate toward plans that hold out the promise of getting it over with, once and for all, in order to live unhindered and uncomplicated lives. Thus, we may expect schemes that promise to minimize testing and struggle always to find a ready hearing among those who long for quick and final solutions to the persistent problems of this earthly journey.

Enter Pride

I have a strong suspicion, based on textual considerations to follow, that Deborah and Barak may well have been set upon by pride. Their victory was astonishing. Now the question was whether God alone would receive the glory.

This should not be an overwhelmingly surprising revelation. Knowing people as we do, and recognizing certain proclivities to which we are all inclined, what better weapon could the Devil employ against a newfound hero? How adept he is at turning the very instruments of blessing against us. He has used it with great success over the centuries. How often have we witnessed a Christian blessed with some recent financial windfall suddenly turn from the church to the country club? Another case in point is the humble, self-effacing fellow who is given the gift of preaching or teaching and, upon experiencing some degree of popularity, becomes an insufferable strutting peacock. Churches and entire denominations are no less susceptible. It is common to find churches that have been blessed with some degree of numerical success declaring themselves to be *the only gospel testimony in the city*. Many of the major denominations, which were born out of great outpourings of the Spirit of God, have become blighted and spiritually sterile as a result of an infusion of pride.

It is when we begin to imagine ourselves, or our group, as immune from being victimized by satanic stratagems that we are at the door of failure. Satan delights in making a shambles of a glowing sanctuary of witness.

The evidence for. our conclusion is drawn from a careful examination of the well-known Song of Deborah found in the fifth chapter of Judges. The song was actually a duet. Deborah sang lead, while Barak provided the harmony. It began well enough, with proper attention given to the power of God. Then Deborah sang, "The inhabitants of the villages ceased, they ceased in Israel, until I, Deborah, arose, arose a mother in Israel" (v 7). After a few more lines, Barak intoned, "Awake, awake, Deborah; awake, awake, utter a song" (v 12). At this point Deborah nudged Barak aside and lifted the melodic reply: "arise, Barak, and lead thy captivity captive, thou son of Abinoam" (v 12). And so it goes.

It seems, indeed, that there are visible threads of pride running through this composition. Confirmation of this is demonstrated by comparing the Song of Moses (Ex. 15), which followed the victory over the hosts of Pharaoh. In it there is not one syllable of mention or recognition of any human being. All praise and recognition are directed to Jehovah in gratitude for His great victory. Not so with the Song of Deborah; she and Barak are very prominent throughout, and the thrust seems to be proper reverence for these who had been merely instruments in the hand of God.

There is a magnificent lesson here. Always beware when one begins to sing about his own accomplishments and memorialize himself with lyrics. Remember, it was the daughters of Israel, not David, who sang, "Saul hath slain his thousands, and David his ten thousands" (1 Sam. 18:7). This temptation can be especially subtle in a day when we have been conditioned to accept groundless bragging and exaggerated claims as facts of life. Unfortunately, many believers seem to have adopted the philosophy that they must *blow their own horns* in order to be noticed. This inevitably leads to the type of unabashed exaggeration and often downright lying used in the process of contemporary image building. The justification for such conduct is to say that the more important one becomes, the more effective he can be in the ministry. Although it is impossible to support this kind of reasoning with a sane, biblical rationale, it is no less than appalling to see the Christian public at large flocking to it. It is a kind of prideful pragmatism that says, *anything, even if it isn't true, to get the job done.*

There are few things more destructive to the effectiveness of Christians than pride. It causes one to become self-centered. It demands that this inflated estimate of self be fed constantly. Furthermore, the larger self becomes, the less important others are. It causes a total reversal of what God designed us to be. We turn from dependence on God to trusting in our own abilities. The glory that is rightly God's is turned toward self, which inevitably causes a breech in fellowship with Him. Other people become instruments to serve self, rather than souls to be served, and the total concept of ministry becomes warped. The result is a life that has lost its usefulness to God and man—a sad picture indeed.

The Remedy

What, then, is the abiding antidote to arrest the fever of pride to which we are all so susceptible? It is present and readily available to all—*a good memory.* Christians are called upon repeatedly in the New Testament to remember certain great facts. Calling them to remembrance serves us well in resisting pride.

The great watchword against pride is found in 1 Corinthians 10:31. Its penetrating message should be memorized by every believer and placed in mental reserve for the Holy Spirit to deploy when we are assailed by the temptation to be proud. "Whether, therefore, ye eat, or drink, or whatever ye do, do all to the glory of God."

Ephesians 2:2 calls upon us to *remember our past*: "Wherefore, remember that ye, being in time past Gentiles in the flesh . . . That at that time ye were without Christ, being aliens from the commonwealth of Israel, and strangers from the covenants of promise, having no hope, and without God in the world" (Eph. 2:11-12).

When we are tempted to become proud, it is beneficial to stop and remember where we were when Christ found us: *without Christ, without promise, without hope, without God*. Here is the bleak picture of the dark pit of misery we occupied apart from Him. When we see afresh the wretchedness we so keenly felt when we knelt to call upon Him for salvation, we rediscover a sense of our unworthiness and His grace. Who among us can be proud of what he was? All redeemed people are, in actuality, *has beens*—thank God! Read the verses again, and rejoice that we are not what we were. As we ponder these precious words, we are reminded of what it took to extricate us from among those who are without hope.

Next, we are encouraged to *remember our position*: "And when he had given thanks, he broke it, and said, Take, eat; this is my body, which is broken for you: this do in remembrance of me. After the same manner also he took the cup, when he had supped, saying, This cup is the new testament in my blood: this do, as often as ye drink it, in remembrance of me" (1 Cor. 11:24-25).

Here we are shown seated with our Savior at the table of fellowship and communion. Remembrance of His shed blood and broken body is emphasized. He magnifies where we are and what it took to get us there. The purchase price required to secure our place at His side is far beyond anything computable in human terms—the suffering and death of the God-Man, Jesus Christ, who was "wounded for our transgressions" (Isa. 53:5). This is another reminder of how low humanity has fallen. There can be no more humbling revelation than this.

There is another side to it also. Redeemed sinners are seated at the table of divine communion garbed with the splendor of heavenly ornamentation. Our garments are fashioned by the hand of God, unsullied by men or angels. We have joined the most exclusive band assembled in the universe of God. And if this tends to reinflate the ego, we should quickly recall that we are here by divine pleasure. It is Christ who has placed us here. The basis of that placement is no more our doing than was Jacob's in receiving the promise. Our right to be at the table is His broken body and shed blood. He who makes any other claim cannot come. We are "accepted in the Beloved" (Eph. 1:6). Our reception, through faith in Him, gives us our standing and assures our eternal state. This being true, what do we have to boast about? Only Christ!

Finally, we are asked to consider our *purpose*—that is, why our Lord has left us in this world: "Wherefore, I will not be negligent to put you always in remembrance of these things, though ye know them, and are established in the present truth" (2 Pet. 1:12). "According to his divine power hath given unto us all things that pertain unto life and godliness, through the knowledge of him that hath called us to glory and virtue" (2 Pet. 1:3).

He reminds us that we have received all things that pertain to life and godliness. These elements combine to make our service productive and attractive. But we are assured that these gifts are ours by virtue of His divine power; we have nothing of which to boast.

The gifted evangelist-theologian-missionary Paul agreed with the foregoing declaration. In his reprimand of the Corinthians for their pride, he stated, "And what hast thou that thou didst not receive? Now if thou didst receive it, why dost thou glory . . . ?" (1 Cor. 4:7). He viewed every ability as a gift from God, something that had been received from God to be used to the glory of God. He claimed to have nothing himself that was not received from the hand of a beneficent Father. If it was true of Paul, how markedly true it is of you and me. Why, then, do we get puffed up about ourselves? It is rather like a bank teller who becomes proud of his benevolence in handing out money that belongs to the bank.

We are expressly told that we are called to *glory* and *virtue*. All true glory, outside God Himself, is reflected glory. If we are functioning properly, we are displaying the reflected glory of our Lord. We are literally lights shining forth in a dark world. Our luminary qualities are transmitters through which men can see God. What a high and holy privilege!

Virtue is said to be ours *by the knowledge of Him*. The building blocks of Christian growth, which bring us to the place of true spiritual living, are ours only as we learn them from Him. To become pharisaically proud of how we live for God is to deny our Lord the credit due Him. Even our virtuous living is but a directional pointer that shows men the way to God.

So we are to remember: remember our *past*; remember our *position*; remember our *purpose*. In so doing, we will have all we need to keep us from falling to pride.

4

GIDEON—The Fearful

GIDEON

The Midianite is in the land,
   Bleak devastation reigns.
Charred fields and looted granaries
   Give witness to their gains.

A lonely figure threshes there
   'Neath Ophrah's grizzled tree,
Then, stunned, he looks
   To find himself in regal company.

The Angel of the Lord, no less,
   Now graces Gideon's view.
"I've come to vanquish all your foes,
   My weapon will be you!"

"My Lord, what instruments have I
   To drive the tyrant hence?"
"Just two, but all sufficient they—
   FAITH and OBEDIENCE."

And the children of Israel did evil in the sight of the LORD; and the LORD delivered them into the hand of Midian seven years. And the hand of Midian prevailed against Israel; and because of the Midianites, the children of Israel made themselves the dens which are in the mountains, and caves, and strongholds (Jud. 6:1-2).

And there came an angel of the LORD, and sat under an oak which was in Ophrah, that pertained unto Joash, the Abiezrite: and his son, Gideon, threshed wheat by the winepress, to hide it from the Midianites. And the angel of the LORD appeared unto him, and said unto him, The LORD is with thee, thou mighty man of valor. And Gideon said unto him, O my Lord, if the LORD be with us, why then is all this befallen us? And where are all his miracles which our fathers told us of, saying, Did not the LORD bring us up from Egypt? But now the LORD hath forsaken us, and delivered us into the hands of the Midianites. And the LORD looked upon him, and said, Go in this thy might, and thou shalt save Israel from the hand of the Midianites. Have not I sent thee? And he said unto him, O my Lord, wherewith shall I save Israel? Behold, my family is poor in Manasseh, and I am the least in my father's house. And the LORD said unto him, Surely I will be with thee, and thou shalt smite the Midianites as one man (Jud. 6:11-16).

So Gideon, and the hundred men who were with him, came unto the outside of the camp in the beginning of the middle watch; and they had but newly set the watch: and they blew the trumpets, and broke the pitchers that were in their hands. And the three companies blew the trumpets, and broke the pitchers, and held the lamps in their left hands, and the trumpets in their right hands with which to blow; and they cried, The sword of the LORD, and of Gideon. And they stood every man in his place round about the camp; and all the host ran, and cried, and fled (Jud. 7:19-21).

And Gideon came to the Jordan, and passed over, he, and the three hundred men who were with him, faint, yet pursuing them (Jud. 8:4).

I T WAS THE TIME OF THE HARVEST in Israel. Fields of ripened grain swayed gently under wafting breezes. The people of the land moved through the golden fields to gather the fruits of their toil.

Suddenly, the vale was swept by high-pitched shrieks and the thunder of camels' hooves. The Midianites! Terrified laborers fled to fortified dens and sullenly watched the invaders load their beasts with the grain the Israelites had tended so patiently. What the Midianite invaders could not carry away they put to the torch. The acrid smell of the burning fields reflected the seared emotions of the people who sowed in hope but would have no harvest.

The scene was all too familiar to the weary descendants of Abraham. It had been reenacted over seven seasons of reaping and had left the inhabitants of Israel on the verge of starvation. So deep were their suffering and humiliation that they raised a unanimous appeal for deliverance to Jehovah.

The Midianites

These were wild, nomadic people who came from the deserts of the east when the waning power of Egypt could no longer sustain protective outposts at the entrance of the Valley of

Esdraelon. The Midianites were descendants of Abraham, through Keturah, whom he had sent away, and they fervently preserved the old animosity toward the sons of Isaac. With the exception of one recorded lapse—the kindness of Jethro, a Midianite, to Moses—their conduct was consistently lamentable.

As tent-dwelling bedouins, they occupied territory with indefinite borders on the east side of the Jordan River. Their intrusions into Israel amounted to far-ranging raids that extended as far as Gaza on the Mediterranean Sea. Guerrilla-type terrorism seemed to be their specialty. Military movements were undertaken during the harvest season to sack the nation's stores. The occupation was not permanent, and no attempt was made to establish governmental authority over the beleaguered Jews. Israel was regarded as a granary that would yield the produce of the land readily enough, at very minimal inconvenience to the marauding invaders.

The devastation of the land is vividly described in the opening verses of Judges chapter 6. A scorched-earth policy accompanied the killing and looting by the Midianites. The sons of Israel were forced to move into dens and caves to ensure their bodily security.

The motivation of the Midianites was twofold: to exploit the resources of Israel, and to reap vindictive pleasure at the affliction brought to the Jews. In the invasion under consideration, they had formed an alliance with the Amalekites, who were ever at the ready to join anyone promising to bring misery to God's chosen people.

While both Israelite and Midianite viewed events from a perspective that was almost exclusively circumstantial, Scripture reveals the causative factors. The roots of the difficulty were not bedded in Egyptian decline, lack of military preparedness on the part of the Israelites, or Midianite bellicosity. Israel, once again, had a handhold on the gods of the former masters of the land. In so doing, they had forged their own fetters. The taproot is laid bare in a statement made through a prophet who came to them by divine behest: "And

I [the LORD] said unto you, I am the LORD your God; fear not the gods of the Amorites, in whose land ye dwell; but ye have not obeyed my voice" (Jud. 6:10). Again, the refusal to obey authored their calamity.

Here we are provided with an excellent view of the incredible variety of satanic implements crafted for the discomfiture of God's people. Their particular method of aggression was not a consistent form of established authoritarianism. It was, rather, a hit-and-run tactic, which allows believers periods of rest and productivity. Then, when we seem to be on the threshold of a rewarding harvest and blessing, a new assault is launched. Each new attack is fashioned to deprive us of the precious fruits of our labors and the accompanying joys. (We shall see shortly, in Gideon, some of the problems this strategy creates.)

You may recall some period in your life when, after an intense period of forcing yourself to be consistent in your devotional life, some protracted illness or other intrusion into the orderly processes of day-to-day life stopped you cold. And, for all of the promises you made to get back to the Book and consistent prayer, you found the struggle even more difficult than it initially was. Thus, Satan capitalizes on those interruptions that are inevitable to inflict lingering spiritual setbacks. It is therefore vital that we understand the purpose of this brutal tactic. It is launched to *confuse, instill fear, and bring deprivation.*

Confusion is brought about by the very nature of the attack. It is initiated from unexpected quarters and falls upon us when everything appears to be progressing well. The intensity seems to be beyond our powers of resistance. Mental frustration mounts with the repetition of the intrusions.

Fear is instilled when it becomes apparent that we are no match for our foe. After we have planned, planted, hoed, and hoped, the enemy, with seemingly ridiculous ease, dashes in to sweep us aside and drive us to our little dens of self-protection. With the offensive gone, fruits stolen, and depression upon us, we begin to wonder if the foe is not, after all, too awesome and powerful to be resisted successfully. Can even God prevent our fondest hopes from being smashed?

71

Satan hopes that this process will deprive us of the final fulfillment of our mission—that of fruit-bearing and reaping. Believers are born to bear: to bear fruit and witness the ends to which God has called us. If the Devil can bring us up short of these objectives, he has partially achieved his purposes.

The Initial Encounter

If Israel was bent on delivering heart and mind to a foreign god, then Jehovah would consign their bodies to a foreign power until they had learned the lessons this form of chastisement is designed to produce. Judges 6:6 announces Israel's arrival at the point of enlightenment: "And Israel was greatly impoverished because of the Midianites; and the children of Israel cried unto the LORD."

The time was ripe for the unveiling of a deliverer who would lead the people from bondage. We are introduced to him as he threshes grain in a winepress at an obscure place called Ophrah. The winepress was chosen in an attempt to elude notice by the Midianites. Our soon-to-be hero beat out his wheat between furtive glances for any sign that would betray the presence of the enemy. As he looked about, he saw an intruder sitting under a nearby oak tree. The startled Gideon found himself in the presence of the angel of the Lord, who addressed him with, what was to Gideon, an unsettling salutation: "The LORD is with thee, thou mighty man of valor" (Jud. 6:12). This greeting reveals that God saw in Gideon much more than he saw in himself. The address was made in the light of yet hidden potential, as opposed to already revealed accomplishments.

Gideon reacted in rather astounding fashion. Rather than prostrating himself in adoration and worship, he blurted out a torrent of questions exposing the depth of his frustration, resentment, and bitterness. If we are startled by his abruptness, we are less so by the familiarity of his questions. "And Gideon said unto him, O my Lord, if the LORD be with us, why then is all this befallen us? And where are all his miracles which our fathers told us of, saying, Did not the LORD bring us up from Egypt? But now the LORD hath forsaken us, and delivered us into the hands of the Midianites . . . And he said unto him, O my Lord, wherewith shall I save Israel? Behold, my family is poor in Manasseh, and I am the least in my father's house" (Jud. 6:13, 15).

It is enlightening to isolate the questions posed by Gideon.

If the Lord be with us . . . ?

Why has all this happened . . . ?

Where are all His miracles . . . ?

How shall I deliver Israel . . . ?

He also threw in a despairing observation: *"But now the LORD hath forsaken us."* Gideon raised four foundational queries. They question the *divine presence, God's purposes, present relevance,* and *personal participation.*

He had heard all that had been said about the presence of Jehovah with Israel in bygone days. The Tabernacle still stood at Shiloh as the "tent of meeting." It declared the perpetual presence of God in the midst of His people. However, the present distress of the nation made it appear to Gideon that the Lord no longer occupied the hallowed sanctuary. If God had been with His people in ancient times, He was surely nowhere to be found in this present day of crisis. He was actually saying, *Where is God when we need Him?*

Gideon raised a timeless issue when he questioned, "Why has all this happened?" Men in all generations have asked the same thing. If God is a benevolent Creator, why does He allow war, famine, and misery to come into the world? Suffering by those who are God's own is even more perplexing. How could Jehovah permit godless men to tower over the people He had chosen? Gideon's question centered on seeking an explanation of God's purpose for the nation. If the people were held in the grip of prolonged persecution, what reason was there for their existence? With circumstances so decidedly against them, it seemed that living for God was a futile affair.

The present relevance of God's working among the people was bitterly questioned. He could not relate the relevance of what had happened in ancient days to what was happening in his lifetime. Youngsters may sit enthralled with the stories told by the bearded elders of the miracles of another era, but if God could hold back the Red Sea and drown the armies of Egypt, why couldn't He stop the unwashed bands of rabble who plagued them? There were no miracles now. If there were ever a time when they were justified, would it not be now?

The terminal point in this rationale is reached in his last statement. Essentially, he said that if God were unable to do anything about it, how could he, Gideon, be expected to accomplish the task? His family was unimpressive, and he was but a stripling. In Gideon's view, the raw material for success simply was not present.

Gideon's resentful fusillade was quietly answered by the divine emissary. He assured Gideon of the Lord's *presence*: "The LORD is with thee" (Jud. 6:12); *purpose*: "Go in this thy might, and thou shalt save Israel from the hand of the Midianites" (Jud. 6:14); and *power*: "Surely I will be with thee, and thou shalt smite the Midianites as one man" (Jud. 6:16). No attempt was made to provide an explanation of the present difficulties. Nor did the Lord address Himself to a rebuttal of Gideon's queries. He simply outlined what He was about to do through His chosen man. For the moment, Gideon would have to be content with these positive statements alone.

With this we are exposed to an element in God's dealing with us that we must all comprehend if we are to live consistent Christian lives. The Lord conveyed to Gideon that He was not concerned, at that juncture, with his understanding of the whys and wherefores of the circumstances. It was, however, vitally important that he *believe God*. That was the overwhelming issue at stake. If he would not believe and learn to trust, even when no explanation was forthcoming, he would not overcome. It was as simple as that. This was to be the first step along the pathway to Gideon's resounding victory over the Midianites. Learning to trust—that was the big thing—coming to the place of such total dependence that he could say, "Though he slay me, yet will I trust in him" (Job 13:15).

We must grasp the fact that it is not always God's design to reveal immediately the reasons for bad circumstances, sickness, or adversity. But while we rest with confidence in the sovereignty of God's prerogatives over our lives, we are to be keenly alert to the present lessons emanating from these situations. They are always there for us to learn, if we will see them. Our problem arises when we become engrossed in the circumstances—trying to find the why, allowing bitterness to take hold when the answer is not swiftly forthcoming. This is especially true during periods of prolonged sickness or distress.

Romans chapter 5 gives important insight: "And not only so, but we glory in tribulations also, knowing that tribulation worketh patience; And patience, experience; and experience, hope" (Rom. 5:3-4). Here we see the all-important fact that tribulation *works*. It works *for* us. It is as necessary to our development as Christians as any other single consideration. Indispensable to our growth is the establishment of a faith that is tried by extremity. Faith is never really tested until difficulty comes. When we are thus assailed and emerge trusting, our walk with God takes on a new dimension.

James added a definitive dimension: "My brethren," he instructed, "count it all joy when ye fall into various trials" (Jas. 1:2). Yes, God allows trials to enter the life of every believer. The purpose, however, is never to tempt or defeat. Every trial has twin purposes: (1) to bring us through and (2) to build us up. For this reason, we can experience joy in trial, even as our Lord, "who for the joy that was set before him endured the cross, despising the shame" (Heb. 12:2).

Brought in to be brought through; brought through to be built up—the concept adds an entirely new objective to all suffering by saints.

Gideon's Fear

Gideon's besetting sin was his inclination to be fearful. It may seem to be a contradictory element in a man who is remembered for his exploits as a warrior. However, the overcoming of his fear gives us an example for our own encouragement.

His fears can be documented quickly. "Alas, O Lord GOD! For I have seen an angel of the LORD face to face" (Jud. 6:22). "Because he *feared* his father's household, and the men of the city, that he could not do it by day, that he did it by night" (Jud. 6:27). "But if thou *fear* to go down, go thou with Purah, thy servant, down to the host" (Jud. 7:10). Additional evidence is gathered by observing his sign-seeking: "Then show me a sign that thou talkest with me" (Jud. 6:17).

It is helpful to observe the repeated assurances given by Jehovah to His trembling servant. In Gideon, deity was confronted with a dual problem: fear and unbelief. What has been interpreted by some as the demonstration of a humble and self-deprecating spirit is, in reality, the manifestation of a lack of faith. It was the reflection of a problem that had to be overcome.

The Fleece

We repeatedly hear people refer to "putting out the fleece" when they are seeking God's direction in some perplexing decision. This, of course, is patterned after Gideon's famous encounter with God in preparation for the engagement with the Midianites. "And Gideon said unto God, If thou wilt save Israel by mine hand, as thou hast said" (Jud. 6:36). We might be less inclined to employ this phrase if we realized that it was a token of Gideon's unbelief (note the "if" in verse 36), rather than his earnestly seeking direction from the Lord. "Behold, I will put a fleece of wool in the floor; and if the dew be on the fleece only, and it be dry upon all the earth beside it, then shall I know that thou wilt save Israel by mine hand, as thou hast said" (Jud. 6:37).

This is a sure evidence that Gideon was having trouble accepting God's revelation to him. The entire episode of the fleece provides a study of divine forbearance and long-suffering.

It is certainly not meant to establish a pattern for others to follow. Gideon felt that he needed a fleece because he did not entirely believe the Word of God!

Our Lord had given complete assurance of victory—He had spoken. That should have been enough. But it was not. Gideon demanded something more. And in his sign-seeking, one act of supernatural manifestation was insufficient; he required a repeat performance.

"And Gideon said unto God, Let not thine anger be hot against me, and I will speak but this once: let me make a trial, I pray thee, but this once more with the fleece; let it now be dry only upon the fleece, and upon all the ground let there be dew" (Jud. 6:39).

The fact that the Lord complied with Gideon's request does not sanctify the process. It merely evidences God's condescending grace toward our persistent doubt.

Gideon's fleece unveils a danger, the seriousness of which modern sign-seekers should be aware. While such elements in Christianity hold out the promise of a deeper spirituality through miraculous manifestations, a lack of spiritual maturity is actually being evidenced. Many who fall prey to these delusive promises find that they become so engrossed in looking for the signs that they become completely diverted from doing what God has called them to do. Spiritual maturity is seen, in its truest sense, when we are able to trust implicitly in the already fully verified witness of the Word spoken by Jehovah. God had said what He would do; it was Gideon's duty to believe and obey.

Go Down, Gideon

Gideon's fear was countered by the application of various components. First, as we have seen, the Lord provided direct assurances through His own Word and working. Next, he raised up a father who would stand with Gideon in his struggle with the foe.

God's first instruction was for Gideon to take some servants and destroy the altar of Baal. This altar belonged to his father and was used in worship by the members of his household and the townspeople. It was no small thing for a son to disgrace his father and family by performing an act of this kind. However, it was to be the first deed of valor on the road to larger things. It would establish the fact that Gideon was putting Jehovah in His rightful place and would thereafter perform all of his exploits in His name and by His power. It was Gideon's public act of consecration to the service of God.

What Gideon expected to occur did not. He was sure that the wrath of his father would fall upon him as a result of the action he was about to take. On the contrary, his father joined him to confront the people, who demanded that Gideon be put to death for destroying the altar and their idol. His father met their belligerence with a severe rebuke: "If he be a god, let him plead for himself, because one hath cast down his altar" (Jud. 6:31). Gideon's decision to stand for God had apparently awakened a sense of spiritual awareness in his father. It may have been that he had been longing for someone to take a step that he did not have the courage to take himself. When Gideon demonstrated his faith, his father was moved to join him, much to Gideon's surprise and delight. This must have been a great source of encouragement.

There is an encouraging, practical word in this experience. Children can lead the way spiritually and bring salvation to lost loved ones and courage to those who are weak in the faith. My own experience bears witness.

Our family was without a significant Christian witness. My father and his brothers had been negatively influenced toward religion early in their lives and, consequently, had been turned off to anything spiritual. It was the persistent effort of a Sunday school teacher to persuade my ten-year-old cousin to attend Sunday school that broke through the dike and brought many in our family to the Lord.

As a result of Cousin Bob's accepting Christ, his father and mother were converted. Uncle Howard joined his son in a witness to my father. Dad and my stepmother trusted Christ and, in turn, witnessed to my wife and me. Since that time the circle of believers, in and out of the family, has grown, and to this day that witness goes on unabated.

It is the type of thing that should inspire those who work among children of unbelieving parents, as well as sons and daughters who seek to lead their parents to the light.

In Gideon's case, the experience initiated at least two things. The response he had feared did not materialize. It was a valuable lesson. It is equally profitable for us. Most of the shadows of fear falling across our paths as Christians never become reality. We live out unsettled days fearing what might happen—it rarely does. His father changed Gideon's name to Jerubbaal: "Let Baal plead against him, because he hath thrown down his altar" (Jud. 6:32). In other words, the enemies of God were suddenly on the defensive. It was now up to Baal to defend himself and make his stand against the one whom God had chosen. Gideon was beginning to learn the power of a faith walk.

Next, God assured Gideon through the appearance of the illustrious *three hundred*. It must have been impressive to see 32,000 men answer the call to arms issued by Gideon. The elation was short-lived. Twenty-two thousand beat a trembling retreat from Mount Gilead when they heard that serious blood-letting was a very real prospect. Of the 10,000 remaining, 9,700 proved to be incompetent and were sent home. The difference between those who returned home and the three hundred who stayed is decisive. Gideon learned that fear is an inherent part of the human mechanism. All of the three hundred knew and experienced a measure of fear. The difference was that they did not succumb to it. It did not become their master. Their fear was committed to God, and He supplied an adequate measure of strength and assurance. Gideon's three hundred would share with him the laurels of victory. "And the LORD said unto Gideon, By the three hundred men who lapped will I save you, and deliver the Midianites into thine hand; and let all the other people go every man unto his place" (Jud. 7:7).

Another important element in Jehovah's provision for Gideon's fear was the presence of a faithful companion to share the conflict. "But if thou fear to go down, go thou with Purah, thy servant, down to the host" (Jud. 7:10). He was being sent to reconnoiter the enemy camp. Purah was sent along as a companion who would share the danger and stand by Gideon. There is great benefit in an association of this kind. God supplied Gideon with a Purah, David with his Jonathan, and Paul with faithful Barnabas. He just as surely sends us companions during our pilgrimage. The joy of fellowship with those who are fellow soldiers of the cross surpasses anything this world can either experience or appreciate. The term *brothers in Christ* can hardly encompass all that comes to us in the persons of true Christian friends.

There is a great need, in our loveless and indifferent world, for believers to make themselves available to others and dare to become a friend sent by God to encourage and strengthen someone. Most of us can remember situations in which we felt dreadfully alone and fearful. How often did the Lord, in His mercy, send someone to our side? Purah was Gideon's *friend in need*.

There was yet one more quieting experience in store for the son of Joash. He was instructed to go down to the camp of the Midianites. The Lord had a word from the enemy for him to hear. As he and Purah crouched outside the tents of the adversaries, an electrifying statement was overheard. A Midianite was relating a dream he had had to his tentmate. The interpretation offered by his disconsolate friend ended with the statement, "This is nothing else except the sword of Gideon, the son of Joash, a man of Israel; for into his hand hath God delivered Midian, and all the host" (Jud. 7:14). The enemy thereby assured Gideon that the battle would be his! He suddenly grasped the fact that the foe had already been defeated and the victory was assured. As he appropriated the divine strategy, triumph was the sure result.

This was the climactic revelation. It is equally so for us today. As we study the Word, we find that Satan is now a defeated foe. "For this purpose the Son of God was manifested, that he might destroy the works of the devil" (1 Jn. 3:8). He is not having a heyday, as we might suppose, but has been met and mastered by our Lord Jesus Christ. Since Calvary, his way has ever been downward. The outcome is not in question. He is plodding toward execution. We need not cower before him in fear. It is true that he possesses great power; however, our Lord has made available to us those instruments that enable us to appropriate His strength and power. The victory is ours; we need not fear.

The scriptural antidote for fear is presented concisely in the 43rd chapter of Isaiah. In light of the problems encountered by Gideon and ourselves, it would be well to spend a moment with this indispensable passage.

> Fear not; for *I have redeemed thee*, I have called thee by thy name; thou art mine. When thou passest through the waters, *I will be with thee*; and through the rivers, they shall not overflow thee; when thou walkest through the fire, thou shalt not be burned, neither shall the flame kindle upon thee. For I am the LORD thy God, the Holy One of Israel, thy Savior; I gave Egypt for thy ransom, Ethiopia and Seba for thee. Since thou wast precious in my sight, thou hast been honorable, and *I have loved thee*; therefore will I give men for thee, and people for thy life. Fear not; for I am with thee. I will bring thy seed from the east, and *gather thee* from the west. I will say to the north, Give up; and to the south, Keep not back; bring my sons from far, and my daughters from the ends of the earth, Even every one who is called by my name; for I have created him for my glory; I have formed him; yea, I have made him (Isa. 43:1–7).

God's answer to man's four greatest fears is given in this text. Initially, He dealt with the fear of *exposure*—that is, being exposed for what we are, as opposed to what we would like others to think we are. Think of the extent to which some people go to ensure that their families and friends will not know their true character. Distasteful habits are hidden from view in an effort to display respectability.

Many go to great lengths to keep the skeletons of the past in well-guarded closets. Psychiatrists and psychologists daily probe the minds of thousands of people who are driven to the brink of emotional disaster by the fear of their past being revealed. Our Lord assures us that He knows us as we really are: "I have called thee by *thy name*" (Isa. 43:1). This implies that the most minuscule areas of our lives are known to Him. All that we do, think, or have been is an open book before Him.

Furthermore, knowing all that there is to know about us, He moves to redeem us through Christ. This is a great mystery, but one that opens the flood gates of revelation regarding the full forgiveness of all of our transgressions. To redeem, in the New Testament sense, means to pay the purchase price in full—literally, to buy out of the slave market, never to return again. As Jesus Christ became our substitute, He was fully exposed to the judgment of God beneath the weight of our sins. When we accept Him as our substitute, that one judgment is viewed by God as sufficient exposure for our transgressions. They will never have to be faced again. As a matter of fact, God not only forgives every sin of a lifetime, but He also forgets them. Judicially, it is as though our sinning never occurred. The songwriter penned accurate words when he wrote of our sins being buried in the sea of God's forgetfulness. This harmonizes with the biblical word, "And their sins and iniquities will I remember no more" (Heb. 10:17).

In the case of sinning saints, we are assured that "If we confess our sins, he is faithful and just to forgive us our sins, and to cleanse us from all unrighteousness" (1 Jn. 1:9). Sin in the life of a Christian is a serious matter. However, when sin is confessed and forsaken, it is stricken from the record, and there is no possibility that we will ever be called to account for it again. Those who continue to be haunted by sins thus confessed should know that it is only Satan who accuses us over past misdeeds, not our Savior.

Next, He addressed Himself to the matter of our fear of *failure*. The reason why so many of us attempt so little for God is the nagging fear of failing in our efforts to serve Him. We see others productively involved for the Lord and envy them. When we look at our lack of abilities, we quickly decide that we had better leave the doing to others who are better equipped. While we reason thus, we fail to appreciate the most significant single factor that makes the difference between success and failure in Christian work. In the passage before us God gives His unequivocal answer for this fear: "I will be with thee" (Isa. 43:2)! Inspiration then details the circumstances under which our Lord promises to be with us. In so doing, He selected the two most extreme conditions in which one may find himself—fire and flood. These are two of the greatest natural disasters that fall upon mankind. They illustrate the worst possible trials we can expect to encounter in this life. Peter desired to walk to the Savior on Galilee and, in the process, began to sink beneath the dark waters. The Lord Jesus reached out to save him. Shadrach, Meshach, and Abed-nego were condemned for their loyalty and service to Jehovah and committed to the furnace. When the startled king looked in, he saw that a quartet had replaced the trio in the midst of the inferno. In both cases, the divine intervention was life-preserving. Both records come to us as testimonies of God's ability and, more importantly, His desire to secure us by His presence.

Ponder the worst that can happen as we launch out for our Lord into the torrent of ridicule or are bitten by the searing flames of opposition. Neither can surmount His promise to be with us. We can literally do anything we are called on to attempt in the will of God.

A church member timidly knocked at the door of a family who had moved into the community. He was invited in and asked to be seated. As he began speaking, it was immediately apparent that he was nearly overcome by fear. He haltingly offered an invitation to the couple to attend the church on Sunday and, without saying much more, left the house. This couple had been visited by others who were eager to have them in their respective churches. When the door closed, the husband turned to his wife and said, "Honey, if that man, as frightened as he was, was willing to force himself to come and invite us to his church, they must have something we're looking for." They visited and, indeed, found in that fellowship what they were seeking in a church home. The point is, our hesitant example believed that God would go before him. In this belief he went and found success.

How wide a range does this cover? It is as far-reaching as our challenges and encompasses every aspect of Christian service. All of our foes, in life and death, are put to flight in His presence.

Third, He addressed our fear of being *unloved*. This is among the great frustrations of our time. Many rush into premature and unfortunate marriages for fear of being passed by and spending boring lives unloved and virtually unwanted. If such is your case, hear the divine Word: "I have loved thee" (Isa. 43:4). Can we explain the full scope of this declaration? Certainly not. But we can accept it and find through it all of the glorious prospects it opens to us.

It is important to recognize that in the love of Christ we have everything we need for time and eternity. His love brings fulfillment and the abundance about which He spoke in the Gospel of John. A friend, Dr. Jimmie Johnson, made the observation that all of us are seeking three basic things: *security, recognition,* and *joy.*

This is an accurate appraisal. The search for security involves our seeking for someone to meet our needs. Recognition reflects our compelling desire to know that someone loves and wants us. Joy is expressive of our yearning for someone with whom we can share, for we come to understand, perhaps ever so slowly, that joy is really, after all, found in giving and sharing.

Now think of it—all of these things are fully experienced as we come to know the love of Christ. He meets our needs; He loves us and wants us for His own; He shares all that He is and all that He has with those who know Him. What more could we ask? All that comes to us by way of human relationships are but glorious fringe benefits, which are the outgrowth of our identification with Him. "Herein is love, not that we loved God, but that he loved us, and sent his Son to be the propitiation for our sins. Beloved, if God so loved us, we ought also to love one another" (1 Jn. 4:10-11).

Finally, He moved to our fear of being *deserted.* One of the most frightening prospects facing those who die without Christ is that they will enter eternal isolation. There will be no fellowship in hell. The tongue-in-cheek banter of worldlings who talk of stoking the furnaces, the dark pleasures to be enjoyed, and the multitudes of companions who will join them are entertaining fanciful delusions. Hell is a place where men will bear their miseries in the perpetual midnight of eternal separation from God and His created beings. It is a chilling fact to contemplate.

Conversely, He gives us the promise that He will, one day, gather those who are His to Himself. "Fear not; for I am with thee. I will bring thy seed from the east, and gather thee from the west" (Isa. 43:5). In death, or at His coming for us, we will meet Him face to face and "ever be with the Lord" (1 Th. 4:17). This is our Savior's great promise. Of course, in context, Isaiah was referring to Israel and the final fulfillment of all the long-sought promises to the ancient people. But the Word rings forth with equal clarity the certainty of Christ's coming for His beloved bride—the Church. For the Christian this means, as Jehovah proceeds to declare, that "thou art mine . . . for I have created him for my glory" (Isa. 43:1, 7). What a striking consideration—*we are His.* The Word proclaims the fact that no matter how insignificant we may feel, He glories in us.

I was visiting the maternity ward of a local hospital some years ago. A lone figure stood positioned before the viewing glass, peering in at the squirming newborns. I stepped quietly up behind the young father, who was too intent to notice my coming. Finally he looked up and proudly inquired, "Do you have one in here?"

"No," I replied.

He looked as though he were introducing me to royalty as he proudly announced, "That one is mine!"

I was immediately reminded of a statement made by Dr. Charles Stevens, for over 45 years the pastor of the Salem Baptist Church in Winston-Salem, North Carolina, to the effect that there are, actually, no newborn infants possessing a compelling physical attractiveness. His method of answering, and staying honest at the same time, was to intone to the parents with careful dignity, "My, what a baby!"

His thesis was well documented in the child I looked down upon. He was wrinkled, red, and bald. Further complicating things was the fact that his skin did not seem to fit. It was much too large for his capacity to fill it. Other babies in that nursery had been in this world long enough to have taken on a reasonably respectable appearance—our subject had a long way to go. This did not make one particle of difference to the beaming father. He was not looking at ugliness; he saw sheer beauty. And we know why. That scrawny infant was his, and he wouldn't have traded it for the universe.

When we look at ourselves and see so much that we do not like, we might wonder how God could want us at all. The overriding factor from the divine side is that we are His, and He sees us in the pure loveliness of our blessed Lord.

This is true because somewhere along the way we have changed our names. The passage begins with Jehovah's statement that He has called us by our name. He concludes by saying, "Even every one who is called by my name" (Isa. 43:7). The real antidote for fear is to change your name to *Christian*. In so doing, all four of these tremendous declarations will be yours.

The Battle

Stand in your places
  With lamps held alighted.
Wait for the trumpet
  To call to the fray.

Stand tall and strong
In the strength of Jehovah.
For His three hundred
Will triumph today!

Gideon's fear was put to rest because God had provided a divine strategy. The implementation of a battle plan was not left to the earthbound commanding general; it had been carefully worked out in Heaven and passed down the ranks. The call now was to implicit obedience. Gideon and his little band were to do what God had instructed, in exactly the way He wanted it done. There would be obstacles in the way— enemies, friends, or self. But, in spite of all that would come, they must obey.

> And he divided the three hundred men into three companies, and he put a trumpet in every man's hand, with empty pitchers, and lamps within the pitchers. And he said unto them, Look on me, and do likewise; and, behold, when I come to the outside of the camp, it shall be that, as I do, so shall ye do. When I blow with a trumpet, I and all that are with me, then blow ye the trumpets also on every side of all the camp, and say, The sword of the LORD, and of Gideon (Jud. 7:16–18).

Our forebear in the faith had taken some long strides in his spiritual evolution. He had reached a position from which he could encourage others to follow his example. This could be stated in the serene knowledge that he was following God. All spiritual growth is bent to this end. When others see Christ in us and therefore have a worthy example to emulate, we are fulfilling God's true purpose for us. "Look on me, and do likewise." Gideon had come far, indeed.

Unfriendly Friends

And the three companies blew the trumpets, and broke the pitchers, and held the lamps in their left hands, and the trumpets in their right hands with which to blow; and they cried, The sword of the LORD, and of Gideon. And they stood every man in his place round about the camp; and all the host ran, and cried, and fled. And the three hundred blew the trumpets, and the LORD set every man's sword against his fellow, even throughout all the host: and the host fled to Beth-shittah in Zererah, and to the border of Abel-meholah, unto Tabbath (Jud. 7:20–22).

The three hundred were not prepared for the treatment they received from their fellow countrymen as they pursued the terror-stricken sons of Midian. One of the most arresting and revealing statements of the entire account is that which says, "And Gideon came to the Jordan, and passed over, he, and the three hundred men who were with him, faint, yet pursuing them" (Jud. 8:4). These faithful stalwarts would see the battle through to victory. They were bone weary and spent for hunger. Most of them were pressed to the limit of their physical and emotional resources. But on they went, doggedly following the chase. As their strength waned, it was apparent that they needed help. The logical place to seek it was from their fellow Israelites, who had born the heat of the Midianite affliction.

Gideon issued an urgent plea to the men of Ephraim to mobilize and cut off the escape route of the fleeing enemies. They did this and captured and dispatched two of the leaders of Midian. There was great cause for rejoicing at this alliance, which held such sound potential for total victory. However, there was to be no joy for Jerubbaal and his weary warriors in this alliance. Ephraim's inflated pride had been injured, and an argument ensued. They remonstrated with Gideon because they had not been consulted or called to the initial engagement. They had been *crushed,* so to speak, at his insensitivity to their feelings. Now the great leader found it necessary to suspend the attack until he could temper the wrath of his wounded friends. He exercised great tact and humbled himself in order to restore a semblance of tranquillity.

In the meantime, the Midianites were stretching their legs to increase the distance between themselves and their uncompromising tormentors. Of course, precious time was lost. Of greater consequence was the damage to the morale of the pursuers, who were getting a look at the fallibilities of their friends.

They next turned to the men of Succoth in search of food. The fare was no better there than it had been at the hands of the men of Ephraim. These men were committed to a compromising course of action. They did not know how the battle was going to turn out; therefore, they were not willing to make any overtures or offer aid until they knew what the result would be. No help would be given until the battle was over. This must have stunned the members of Gideon's force. They were totally bewildered by such blatant indifference. One could well have understood it if they had laid spears on shoulders and retired to their homes.

The men of Penuel only added insult to injury by confirming that they, too, would await the outcome of the contest. All of these reactions served to prove that there were many more cowards than courageous men in Israel.

The illustrations gathered from these encounters are as fresh as every rising generation. If we are learning that the judges were ordinary men, we are also seeing that people in general never change much either. The problem types only change clothing and languages. Wherever believers are found, one can expect the same manifestations. Surprisingly, some of the most heated opposition to stepping out for God comes from those who profess Christ. Many who have been called to Christian work have found, to their astonishment, that it was members of their own families and intimates who offered the most discouragement. Therefore, in Christian work opposition can be expected from friends as well as foes. While this may be difficult to understand, it is, nonetheless, a fact of life.

Compromisers are always a source of frustration and trial. Those who wish to keep one foot in the world and the other in the church door ever attempt to impede the progress of the separated saints. They equivocate over every effort to take a firm public stand on the issues of morality and witness for Christ.

They are rather like the minister who was a member of a preachers association in which there was a move afoot to oppose the sale of alcoholic beverages in the county. After long deliberations and lengthy statements about the strong leadership the clergy must take on this issue, an affirmative vote was delivered. As the president began to instruct the secretary to notify the press, the hand of this prominent clergyman shot skyward. After being recognized, he counseled that, although he was foursquare behind the declaration, he didn't feel it was the kind of thing that should be made public. He preferred to work behind the scenes through, in his words, *the still-small-voice approach*, thereby avoiding any criticism by members of the community who favored public tippling.

This type of attitude is a sore affliction to the Church. We must recognize, however, that we will always have such people among us. The minister who flays his faithful few week in and week out, in an attempt to alter the conduct of some absent spiritual ne'er-do-wells, makes a serious error. If they do not respond to the positive challenges of the Word and the exhilaration of the contest, we can expect little response to our *skinning them*. It may cause the minister some degree of comfort for having *got 'em told*, but the larger effect is to dishearten eager believers who need spiritual nourishment.

Gideon's three hundred resisted the temptation to lose the fruits of their triumph because of those who stood in the way. They had a quality that caused them to keep their eye on the larger purpose of their mission. They also possessed that rare perception that enabled them to see who the real enemy was and not to become so busy in controversies with friends that they allowed the foe to escape. Thus, the greater enemy, Satan, was deprived of one of his most successful and often-used weapons when the people of God are on the move.

God used a few men to secure peace for the many. It was always the remnant in Israel who settled the great controversies and provided spiritual thrust for the nation. This has been historically true in the life of the Christian Church. Those who dare to believe and obey have always been in the vanguard of the assaulting forces moving against the citadels of Satan. The great commentary on their effort was that the land had rest for forty years. The Midianites were crushed and were no longer a serious threat to the tranquillity of Israel. This in itself was reward enough for God's tireless warriors.

The Outgrowth Problem

Gideon's triumph was rooted in implementing the strategy God had developed. He relied on Jehovah to allay his fears and guide him in accomplishing a military feat, the magnitude of which has seldom been equalled. This brought him instant popularity. In fact, there was a clamor raised for him to become king and to establish a dynasty in Israel. "Then the men of Israel said unto Gideon, Rule thou over us, both thou, and thy son, and thy son's son also; for thou hast delivered us from the hand of Midian" (Jud. 8:22). He resolutely resisted these pressures and declared that it would be the Lord who would rule over the nation.

Without so much as a murmur of prayer for direction from God, Gideon announced his own strategy. He had what he thought would be the answer for the people. He had carefully pondered the problem and was ready to implement a lasting solution. Albeit quite unconsciously, Gideon took the direction of the nation out of the hands of God and placed it in his own frail capacities. Sincerity was never a question; he simply felt that, because God had directed him to great heights, he would be able to chart the future effectively.

The Ephod

"And Gideon made an ephod thereof, and put it in his city, even in Ophrah: and all Israel went there playing the harlot with it, which thing became a snare unto Gideon, and to his house" (Jud. 8:27).

Gideon requested that the conquerors bring earrings from the spoil they had taken, along with various gold implements seized from their enemies. "And Gideon said unto them, I would desire a request of you, that ye would give me every man the earrings of his spoil. (For they had golden earrings, because they were Ishmaelites.)" [Jud. 8:24]. He apparently intended to create an object to represent the perpetual reign of Jehovah over the people of Israel.

An ephod was a priestly garment worn as part of the high priest's vestments. Gideon's ephod was a replica fashioned from the gold and jewels contributed from the spoils of war. We can only speculate as to his full intent in casting this object. It may well be that the earrings were prominent as a reminder that Israel was to keep an ear open to the commands of God. That it was made from the spoils taken from the enemy could signify the supremacy of Jehovah over the opposing nation and its gods. The fact that it was associated with the priesthood and called to mind the worship of God was most certainly meant to indicate that it was God who was sovereign over the nation and that they must ever follow Him.

These points were all very logical in the mind of Gideon. However, God was not in it, and the end result was that the people, so recently severed from the old gods, saw in it the opportunity to adopt another image to worship. They promptly did this and became ensnared in the idolatry that endured for years to come. Gideon had played squarely into the hands of Satan in his attempt to give the nation continuing guidance.

His problem, then, was brought about by replacing divine strategy with human wisdom. How easy it is to fall into this trap. The Lord's guidance is replaced with our emerging feeling that we need not bother God by asking Him to supply solutions to problems we are capable of working out for ourselves. While we do not articulate this, it is what we, in fact, begin to do. And when we do, we are prone to make grave errors in judgment that can lead us, and those who have developed confidence in our leadership, into serious and prolonged difficulties.

The Remedy

The answer to this dilemma is to reapply the principle we dealt with in our study of Barak—*remembrance*. Think back periodically and see from where we have come. This always bears reapplication.

Then, we must add *reliance* to our weaponry. Had Gideon continued to rely on God for direction and counsel, he would never have fallen victim to such a grievous infraction. Reliance has three fundamental elements, all of which are indispensable if we are to go on after gaining initial victories.

First, there is the matter of staying close to the Word of God. This may seem to be repetitious, but it is no less necessary. The problem accompanying any degree of prominence is that we tend to become busy people. Consequently, those who have demonstrated some capacity for spiritual leadership soon find that they are taxed to the limit of their powers to meet all of the responsibilities thrust upon them. This allows less time to get into the Word and obtain food for the soul. There is no consistent guidance apart from the Word of God. The Holy Spirit and the Scriptures always work in concert with each other. When we begin to neglect the Word, we find that the guidance of the Spirit becomes less definite. Before long, spiritual decisions are being made in the energy of the flesh, and when this occurs, failure is never far behind.

Reliance on the leadership of the Holy Spirit is the next matter to consider. If we do not have clear leadership on a given direction to pursue, we had better wait until we receive it. We are, in a sense, nearly obsessed with hurry these days. We reason that there is not much time left to us, so we had better be doing something. While there is certainly an element of truth in this line of reasoning, it is preferable to take enough time to be sure that what we are doing is not the wrong thing. Then we should develop the kind of patience that allows us to seek positive direction from the Spirit. Those who fall prey to the tyranny of hurry find it a demanding taskmaster. Proper exploration of open avenues is a vital consideration. Look to the Spirit for assurance as you weigh all possible alternatives.

Reliance upon patient, believing prayer is the third corner of the triangle. It is the factor that brings total balance to the business of continual reliance on God. We must never permit prayer to become a distant, formal exercise. Maintaining a vibrant prayer life is perhaps the most taxing element in the Christian discipline. Prayer is offensive to our old nature. Consistency, and particularly prolonged periods of intercession, are therefore stubbornly resisted by the flesh. It is often hard work to pray. In this day, when we are constantly assailed by proponents of the *happiness syndrome,* we begin to feel very unspiritual if everything we do is not accompanied by scintillating surges of happiness. We must not be deluded. Consistency involves discipline; discipline involves repetition; repetition is something most of us seek to avoid when we can.

Two considerations assist us at this point: the nature of the opposition and the nature of the promise. The fact that there is such resolute opposition to consistent prayer—and consistency in prayer is the key to effective living—serves to emphasize the importance of it. Satan's untiring efforts to thwart our resolve to pray betray his deep-seated fear of our having intimate communion with our Lord.

The promise is trumpeted with unquestionable clarity: "And all things, whatever ye shall ask in prayer, believing, ye shall receive" (Mt. 21:22). The importance of this word cannot be denied. It is fundamental to obtaining every provision God has made for us—physical, spiritual, and vocational. All hindrances to its fulfillment are from the human side. It is there for us to receive. We must exercise ourselves in believing appropriation of this overwhelming promise.

The basic requirement is to keep at it. In times of great stress or relative ease, busy or idle, sought out to perform large tasks or buried in near obscurity, we must constantly rely on the power of prayer if we are to experience the guidance so essential to being overcomers.

Our reliance, then, must be on the Word, the guidance of the Holy Spirit, and a consistent prayer life. In these essentials we find the enduring remedy against being victimized by employing human wisdom rather than relying on our great God.

5

JEPHTHAH—The Forsaken

JEPHTHAH—THE FORSAKEN

They cried for God to send a man
   To slay cruel Ammon's hand.
He'd made his boast and then swept down
   To claim Jehovah's land.

Their hero by design must know
   Bold courage, virtue, truth.
Be of a proper heritage;
   Twice blessed with strength and youth.

God made His choice and shocked them all
   When He revealed His aim
To use a harlot's outcast son,
   One Jephthah was his name.

"But Lord, there must be someone else.
   We drove that scoundrel thence."
That "scoundrel" has what you yet lack—
   FAITH and OBEDIENCE.

Now Jephthah, the Gileadite, was a mighty man of valor, and he was the son of an harlot: and Gilead begot Jephthah. And Gilead's wife bore him sons; and his wife's sons grew up, and they thrust out Jephthah, and said unto him, Thou shalt not inherit in our father's house; for thou art the son of a strange woman. Then Jephthah fled from his brethren, and dwelt in the land of Tob: and there were gathered worthless men to Jephthah, and went out with him. And it came to pass, in process of time, that the children of Ammon made war against Israel. And it was so, that when the children of Ammon made war against Israel, the elders of Gilead went to fetch Jephthah out of the land of Tob. And they said unto Jephthah, Come, and be our captain, that we may fight with the children of Ammon. And Jephthah said unto the elders of Gilead, Did not ye hate me, and expel me out of my father's house? And why are ye come unto me now when ye are in distress? And the elders of Gilead said unto Jephthah, Therefore we turn again to thee now, that thou mayest go with us, and fight against the children of Ammon, and be our head over all the inhabitants of Gilead. And Jephthah said unto the elders of Gilead, If ye bring me home again to fight against the children of Ammon, and the LORD deliver them before me, shall I be your head? And the elders of Gilead said unto Jephthah, The LORD be witness between us, if we do not so according to thy words. Then Jephthah went with the elders of Gilead, and the people made him head and captain over them; and Jephthah uttered all his words before the LORD in Mizpah (Jud. 11:1–11).

THE SPECTER OF SCANDAL had fallen upon Ramoth-Gilead. Rumor had it that one of the village's leading citizens had become involved in an illicit affair with a local woman of the street. Ramoth-Gilead was a place where there were few secrets, and bad news traveled fast. One might suppose that the local gossips went early to fill their water pots at the public well and lingered long in order to savor every sordid morsel as it was brought to light.

One by one the seamy details became known, and it was soon evident that the rumor was true. Gilead had been publicly named as the father of a child being carried by a common prostitute. He would take full responsibility for his act, and when the infant was born he would take it into his home to raise as a member of his household. His wife had mixed emotions about this and may have bitterly resented the patronizing attitude of the women of the village toward her as she endured the months before the arrival of the child.

At long last the new arrival was brought into the home. His father promptly named him Jephthah and settled down to the business of raising a boy who would be marked for life by the emblem of his father's shame.

In the process of time, other sons were born and took their places in the family circle. Jephthah learned soon enough that their coming was not a cause for him to rejoice, because from their first glimmer of awareness of the circumstances surrounding his birth, they looked upon him as unworthy of the family name. As the animosities between the young men heightened, Gilead's health declined, and it became evident that he would not live to see his sons enjoy the fruits of their manhood.

The demise of Gilead brought the smoldering family conflict into bitter confrontation. When the issue of the inheritance was to be settled, Jephthah's bastardy was thrown in his face by his half brothers. Not only did they deny him any claim to his inheritance, but they drove him out of the household, thus denying him bed and board as well. "And Gilead's wife bore him sons; and his wife's sons grew up, and they thrust out Jephthah, and said unto him, Thou shalt not inherit in our father's house; for thou art the son of a strange woman" (Jud. 11:2).

He apparently made an appeal to the elders of the city, but to no avail. "And Jephthah said unto the elders of Gilead, Did not ye hate me, and expel me out of my father's house?" (Jud. 11:7). They, at least tacitly, ratified the decision of the brothers. In deciding in favor of Jephthah's brothers, the city fathers forfeited their solemn responsibility to protect the innocent and dispense justice with an even hand. They fell into the old trap of making the son pay for the disreputable conduct of his father. In so doing, they joined the sanctimonious village snobs in opposing a youth who was guilty of nothing except being born. The circumstances of his conception and birth branded him as an undesirable with members of the family and community. The injustice of this attitude is all too evident. The fact that the leaders of the village dignified it by their approval only adds to the magnitude of the offense.

How many times has history witnessed the repeat of this cycle? Those born with *trashy parentage* or *bad blood* are often rejected without a trial. They are destined to live under the mantle of the transgressions of others.

So Jephthah, stung by public humiliation, fled the community and drifted to the north. His immediate motivation was, understandably, to put as much distance as possible between himself and his arrogant brothers. The journey took him to a place called Tob, a city northeast of Ramoth-Gilead.

Into the Caldron

Jephthah was consigned to make his way as best he could. One can well understand how resentment may have caused him to want to strike out and even the score. Consequently, he gathered about him a group of "worthless fellows" and became a freebooting soldier of fortune. We are not given details about these "worthless fellows" who became Jephthah's companions, but their crushing victory over the Ammonites confirmed their stature as fighting men. Jephthah's troops may have been of the same cast and character as David's "mighty men" (2 Sam. 23:8), who were not "worthless" people but who had been cast off by society because of bad circumstances. "And every one who was in distress, and every one who was in debt, and every one who was discontented, gathered themselves unto him [David]; and he became a captain over them" (1 Sam. 22:2).

While we are not told the precise nature of Jephthah's activities, some authorities believe that he was engaged in guerrilla warfare against the Ammonites, who were oppressing Israel at the time. At any rate, he became so accomplished at whatever he was doing that his reputation was soon widely known. Apparently he had a rude sort of fierceness about him that may have been an outgrowth of his resentment over past injustices. No doubt the years intensified the feeling of frustration he bore over being an outcast. Satan no doubt attempted to exploit his past during this period in order to so embitter him that any consideration of usefulness for God would be forever driven from his mind.

We can be sure that he was frequently assailed by what could be called an *oddball complex*. This has been a favorite and most successful instrument in the hand of our wily enemy. In Jephthah's own mind, he was one of a kind. His mother was a harlot, his father disgraced. Indeed, he had experienced a bad start in life. His earliest memories had been linked with the consequences of an act of shame. The results were no doubt a deep-seated insecurity and a feeling of inferiority, which would crop up from time to time throughout the remainder of his life. The fact that he had been viewed as unworthy even to associate with *decent people* seared the brand of rejection deep into his consciousness.

The pathetic tragedy of feeling scorned and rejected is not confined to ancient days. One of the most common modern manifestations is seen in those who resort to the divorce courts to solve husband-and-wife problems. In these days of self-obsessed lifestyles, too often people are encouraged to quit a marriage if they feel they can no longer "cope." Many enter marriage with the feeling that if things don't work out to their satisfaction, they will simply change mates. When children are involved the results can be devastating, for while the adult sees it as a solution—perhaps an opportunity to satisfy the desire for promiscuous living—the child experiences a problem he must relate to for the rest of his life. He has been rejected. No matter how the guilty parent justifies the decision to leave, when the door closes behind a departing mother or father the child experiences the excruciating feeling of being somehow unworthy and rejected. The emotional impact cannot be measured in law books or counseling guides; the result is traumatic and enduring.

Satan's emissaries have long used this divide-and-conquer tactic to convince their victims that they really are, after all, different from others around them. They have problems that are unique to their case. Consequently, they feel beset by abnormal temptations that they feel no one else experiences in quite the same way. When one comes to this conclusion, he is far along the road to falling to the *oddball complex*. The symptom is particularly evident among those who have not been raised in good spiritual circumstances or who have lived lives marked by gross sin. Those who have lived *on the other side of the tracks* frequently experience this feeling. They are tempted to accept a spiritually inferior status and settle down on a plain somewhat below that of the more advantaged Christian.

I remember a man who was reared in very poor circumstances. He was acutely aware of his poverty and, as a result, became very self-conscious about it. As a young man he made a profession of faith and began to attend church. One Sunday, he was chided mercilessly by an unthinking churchgoer for attending worship wearing common clothes—he happened to be wearing bib overalls, which was all his family could afford. He was so embarrassed by this experience that he left the church, never to darken the door again. No amount of explanation or encouragement could ever change his mind. One may object on grounds that he should have been above such a strong reaction to a rather insignificant episode. Perhaps so, but the irresolvable attitude I confronted over years of working with him as a pastor demonstrated that the criticism dealt him a blow from which he never recovered. Such is the lurking power of self-consciousness over being *different*.

We further compound the problem when we turn those who have lived lives characterized by sinful abandon into Christian oddities who are dragged from church to church, or city to city, to give their testimonies about sordid pasts as thieves, murderers, drunkards, or former specialists in some nefarious enterprise. Thinking Christians have been concerned over the recent development of what amounts to a church-related vaudeville-type circuit. If one travels occasionally, he will see the same people advertised by churches across the country as having come to give their testimony. The more sensational the billing, the more appealing it seems to be. No doubt many churches are filled by those who wish to hear these people detail past transgressions.

To be sure, testimonies by people *who have been there* can be a vital encouragement to others who are in the same situation and need Christ. But Spirit-directed sensitivity must be exercised to ensure that those who attend are there to thrill to the grace of God rather than to receive a vicarious *high* from excessive detail about sinful acts. Exploiting the pasts of people already inwardly plagued by insecurities about what they were or where they came from can result in tragedy. Following are some reasons why this is true.

1. Detailing sins of the past, particularly in sexual areas, makes an insidious appeal to fleshly curiosity, which excites unwholesome responses in the thought lives and actual conduct of some hearers. Problematically, explicit sexual fare is becoming increasingly popular among contemporary Christians—a few hours listening to "Christian" talk shows or browsing through bookstores tend to confirm this. We are currently experiencing a revolution in sexually explicit attitudes and materials. The Apostle Paul set the boundaries in this area with some explicit words of his own. Believers are to major in wholesome, loving, disciplined, sacrificial living. "But," he warned, "fornication, and all uncleanness, or covetousness, let it not be once named among you, as becometh saints" (Eph. 5:3). The apostle further admonished, "And have no fellowship with the unfruitful works of darkness but, rather, reprove them. *For it is a shame even to speak of those things which are done of them in secret*" (Eph. 5:11-12). Many Christians are hearing and conducting casual conversations in areas that can end in spiritual and moral disaster.

2. The individual so involved is made to feel that the most important thing he has ever done is to have been a *big* sinner. Appealing to the notion that those who promote him are glorifying the grace element in his salvation does not nullify the fact that they are, in fact, resorting to shoddy spectacularism in order to make an appeal or draw a crowd.

3. The poor chap who was raised in a godly home, went to church and Sunday School, accepted Christ at an early age, and never wallowed in the quagmire of degrading conduct is made to feel that he doesn't have a very effective testimony. The evidence of this seems to be confirmed when he is passed over in favor of someone who has *lived*. How often have we

heard the remark, which is utter nonsense, that those who have lived in deep sin make better Christian workers as a result of their past?

4. Although he may not realize it, being thus exploited is spiritually demeaning to the person exposed in this manner. When he is made a sin specialist, he is, in effect, set apart from other believers. This tends to deepen the *oddball complex,* which in turn inhibits natural, rounded growth in the Christian life. The past is only a thing to be remembered as we appreciate what our Lord in His mercy has done for us. It should be categorized with *forgetting those things which are behind.* When one is called upon to detail his past life time after time, we should not be surprised when backsliding occurs, as it often does with people in this position. By not allowing them to forget past inclinations and weaknesses, we are aiding in their possible regression.

One must wonder about some of the entertainers who have made professions of faith only to turn back to the world after years or only months of association with the Church. It goes without saying that many of these people were attempting to broaden their appeal or simply, as some have confessed, experiencing "the gospel phase of my career." One must wonder, however, how many of these people have found themselves in the clutches of "Christian" promoters who exploit their names and talents to a point where life is about the same as before they professed faith, but with Jesus tacked on. Only eternity will reveal the answer to this. In the meantime, we must lament any infant Christian who is exploited and whose spiritual growth is stunted by people who should have been uplifting encouragers.

The Scripture admonishes us to concentrate on those things that are constructive and growth-inducing: "Finally, brethren, whatever things are true, whatever things are honest, whatever things are just, whatever things are pure, whatever things are lovely, whatever things are of good report; if there be any virtue, and if there be any praise, think on these things" (Phil. 4:8).

The past should always be viewed from the strict perspective of God's redeeming grace. The Christian community should, of course, never be guilty of applying a standard of residual guilt to those who have become members of the body of Christ. He is the great leveler of men. We have all been rightly judged guilty by God. Our defection varies only by degree. We deserve to be cut off from God. Yet, in His grace, He stooped to save and make all believers one in Him (Eph. 2:11–22). We are members of the family and heirs of the promises. This one consideration alone causes Christianity to tower majestically above all man-made religions.

Occasionally, however, we find those who carry discrimination over into the church. How sad it is to find some catered to and favored, while others are passed by and relegated to a kind of second-class citizenship. Churches where community leaders and the wealthy are placed in positions they are not spiritually qualified to fill are writing a sure obituary of their power with God.

There is another, more subtle manifestation of which we should take note. This is found in churches whose members seem to derive hyperspiritual satisfaction in making it difficult to become a member of their particular assembly. They have elaborate programs by which prospective members must prove themselves before they are allowed to enter the local fold.

Placing obstacles in the way of infant Christians is extremely difficult to justify in the light of the New Testament record of the first-century institution to which were "added . . . daily such as should be saved" (Acts 2:47). Christian brotherhood means being accepted in the beloved. A new convert should not be born with a question mark over his head. Most people with unfortunate backgrounds who profess faith in Christ have been on some kind of probation most of their lives. It seems ill-advised to afflict them with more of the same.

Too often the church comes across as desiring to see if the prospective member can measure up to the self-proclaimed spiritual level of those already *in*. It is the sort of attitude that would say to an infant, "When you can live on an adult plain and prove that you are able to participate without causing too many problems for the family, we will apply for your birth certificate and consider giving you our name." This spirit is the attitude employed by the Pharisees, which we all roundly, and rightly, condemn.

The church is the place for spiritual babes. It is an institution created by our Lord to deal effectively with our problems in growth and nurture. The fear that we may allow someone to pass our portals with growth problems by which we are not ready to be challenged might be an admission of our own spiritual ineptitude.

Our view in no way endorses or promotes *easy believism* or undisciplined churches. Every church must have a thorough program in doctrine and training for new converts and members. New Testament standards of discipline should be clearly enunciated and applied. But the objective is that acceptance into the church be based on a clear profession of faith in Jesus Christ. Teaching, training, and exercising discipline are to be carried on within the membership. Above all, we must never discourage babes in Christ by appearing to be sanctimonious know-it-alls eager to reject those who do not appear to be in our spiritual class.

"Then Jephthah fled from his brethren, and dwelt in the land of Tob" (Jud. 11:3). Is it any wonder that Jephthah took to the hills in sulking disgust and confusion? He had been betrayed by his brothers. Worse still, he had been turned on by those leaders who were pledged to his protection. We must wonder how many have left our churches with similar misgivings.

Jephthah would bear the full brunt of humiliation and loneliness that is the lot of the outcast. In Tob he would pass his days with his worthless companions who, like himself, had been turned out by family and town. It matters little why they were cast out; their individual stigmas brought them together in a fellowship of rejects.

There's a wonderful phrase in Judges 11:4 that unveils a masterstroke in God's plan to nurture and heal hurting saints:

"And it came to pass, *in process of time*, that the children of Ammon made war against Israel." By the time the Ammonites made their ill-advised move against Israel, the Lord had prepared His man for the moment of crisis. "In process of time"—that was the critical factor. As Jesus would later call His buffeted band to "Come aside . . . and rest a while" (Mk. 6:31), so Jephthah was taken aside for a time of healing and preparation. It was crucial for the harlot's son to allow time and the gracious hand of God to set things right in his life.

Sooner or later, every generation of saints must learn to wait—wait for God to do what only He can and come to grips with the fact that there are no quick fixes for some of life's bumps and bruises. There must, of necessity, be a "process of time" during which we can experience the Lord's provision for healing. This is additionally difficult for a generation that demands an instant answer for every dilemma. Although it may seem that there are no tomorrows unless our problems are solved before sundown, there are always tomorrows for those who walk with Him, and He will properly prepare us for every contingency—"in process of time."

The Cutting Edge

"When my father and my mother forsake me, then the LORD will take me up" (Ps. 27:10).

More was going on in Tob than met the physical eye. While one might be inclined to write off any spiritual possibilities for one so deeply scarred, the divine hand was about the business of cutting and shaping a responsive character. The result of the surgery would be a life placed at the disposal of Jehovah.

There is a very special place in the heart of God for the outcast. The proof of this is in the fact that He has used so many to mold the course of history. Our Lord is not subject to the shallow judgments by which we are often victimized as we evaluate our fellowmen. He always judges according to actual potential rather than the peripheral measurements so often employed by humans. Jephthah was a man who was forced to walk virtually alone. He avoided and was avoided by his peers. But it was this very situation, which on the surface was so unfortunate, that exposed a divine opportunity.

Often it is in the barrenness of enforced isolation that minds and hearts are thrown open to God. As a result, a single-hearted devotion and loyalty develop, which are rooted in this solitary involvement with Jehovah. It is often the time when God does something very special in the lives of His children.

Who among us has not chaffed under some period of isolation that seemed to be utterly wasted time? Some years ago, while I was pastoring a rapidly growing church, my doctors suspected that I had developed a heart problem. Following weeks of enforced inactivity, I was dispatched to a hospital some distance from home for extensive evaluation. For a week, specialists tested and conferred about my condition. Finally they performed a heart catheterization, which they hoped would supply an explanation of my problem.

Their report, much to my relief, was that there was no problem with the heart at all. The difficulty was from a much less serious source. I was relieved, yes, but also puzzled and a bit disturbed. With so much to be done and no time for this sort of thing, why had I been forced into a week of totally unproductive solitude—wasted time?

Fortunately, I was allowed a privilege that some never receive. I was favored to see just why I had been forced into a situation where necessary activity gave way to specific spiritual productivity, for to wile away my time in the hospital and alleviate boredom, I wrote three poems about Jerusalem. Those poems later were distributed among Jewish leaders in the United States and Israel. They were enthusiastically received and served to open many important doors for future research and writing. That "wasted" week of isolation was, in fact, among the most productive weeks of my life.

Isolation was a valuable instrument in the experience of the Apostle Paul. Following his conversion to Christ, he was rejected by his former companions and held suspect by many

Christians. In those circumstances God instructed him to retire to Arabia for three years of solitude (Gal. 1:15–18). God used these years to inculcate the great theological concepts that have been the bedrock on which the Church has been built. When he left the confines of that single communion, he was thrust into the arena of activity and controversy. The record of his accomplishments for our Lord demonstrates the effectiveness of the Spirit-directed training program.

Such appears to have been the case with Jephthah. Somehow, over the years, he came into an intimate relationship with the Lord. The qualities we have commended throughout this book—faith and obedience—were developed to a high level in Jephthah. In his exchanges with the king of Ammon he demonstrated an intimate knowledge of the Pentateuch. The Word of God had become a vital force in his life.

Lack of specific information prevents us from looking deeper into this matter, but we must wonder if somewhere along the way Jephthah met some loyal, godly person who had an abiding concern for the souls of men—someone who took the time to explain the fallibilities of man and the majesty of the grace of God to this wounded judge, one who was willing to spend patient hours expounding the great truths of God's Word.

It is interesting to speculate about who such a man may have been. Was it his penitent father who spent his precious remaining years instructing his son in the things of God? Perhaps. Or it may have been one of the men who came to Jephthah's side during the long years of exile in Tob. One thing we know: If such a man existed, and we can be virtually certain he did, he must have been a man in whom Jephthah saw a glorious contradiction to what he had observed in others who claimed religion. There must have been a spiritual virility and consistency that sparked the flame that would later burn in his own soul. And this nameless ambassador of Jehovah must assuredly have been blessed with persistence. In Jephthah he found a man smarting under the lash of hypocritical injustices. He would be a hard nut to crack. We can only guess at how many rebukes, insults, and perhaps even threats were endured by this man before the light began to break in Jephthah's soul.

But we can well give pause to thank God for all such singularly invaluable individuals who are willing patiently to ply the byways of life seeking out those for whom Christ died. They sing through the open-air meetings on crowded city streets. You will find them quietly working among those who are incarcerated. Missions, rehabilitation centers for wayward youth, Christian agencies for alcoholics and addicts, homes for the elderly, crisis pregnancy centers—all know them well. They are unsung and seldom hear the accolades of the masses, but, we can agree, they are true heroes of the faith.

Whatever means God chose to use, it is evident that the divine provision met Jephthah's personal need. The one who was turned out by his fellows grew into a refreshing person under the hand of God. And when God sought a man to use against the ancient foes of His people, He chose the harlot's son! God was more interested in the man than where he had trained. He was more concerned with his capacity for tenacity and courage than for theological acumen. This is not to disparage institutions or the need for studious, godly theologians and expositors. It is to say emphatically that God has a place for each of His children to fill, and when He needs a man, He chooses the one best suited to fill the place of responsibility to His glory. The Lord was not, after all, concerned about where Jephthah had come from. He was concerned about where he was going—to the glory of God.

In the final analysis, Jephthah came into the spotlight as one tempered to believe and obey. He was a man prepared by Jehovah to perform a task his contemporaries could not handle. In the loneliness of Tob he had developed into a resolute, bold, and resourceful individual. When necessity beckoned, he was ready to step out of the wings and face the enemy.

It is interesting to observe how God worked through Jephthah. He did not receive a celestial strategy, as did Gideon.

Nor was he the beneficiary of direct divine intervention, as had been the case with Barak. No! Our Lord was once again tailoring the provision to answer the personal problem. This time it was to be in forthright confrontation. His former tormentors would petition him for his favor and leadership. "And it was so, that when the children of Ammon made war against Israel, the elders of Gilead went to fetch Jephthah out of the land of Tob. And they said unto Jephthah, Come, and be our captain" (Jud. 11:5–6). They humbly agreed to his terms for becoming their deliverer (Jud. 11:7–11). His worth to the program of God and his worthiness before his people were thus firmly established. He was adequately compensated for the years of suffering under the bitter stigma of rejection by his own. God's higher purposes began to take shape before him. He began to appreciate the value of patience during his own period under the supreme Schoolmaster. He saw that while God was preparing him, He was also teaching Israel. Now the twin processes converged and both parties were able to see clearly.

Balancing the Books

"Vengeance belongeth unto me, I will recompense, saith the Lord. And again, The Lord shall judge his people" (Heb. 10:30).

All accounts will be fully and finally settled by God. Our bitterness and fretting only prove to be self-defeating. Satan and his cohorts are quick to grasp the advantage over us when we struggle under the burden of resentment.

Jephthah had been wronged. His brothers had carefully calculated the misery they gleefully visited upon him. They were back in Gilead enjoying the fruits of the inheritance in which he should have shared. We do not know how much Jephthah knew about what was happening in his homeland while he was away. We are, however, blessed with a view that shows both sides of the coin.

Things back home were not as Jephthah might have imagined them to be. The Ammonites had increasingly oppressed the people of Gilead until the situation had become desperate. They were now virtual chattels of the invaders. The brothers of Jephthah, who had so viciously dealt with him, found that the Ammonites were adroit at dealing them more of the same. Their own devices were now leveled against them, and they were under the threat of being disenfranchised. They were learning the hard way.

God has pledged Himself to rectify injustices. It is never a matter of *if*, only a question of *when* and *how*. He is the guardian of His people. When oppressors raise threatening hands against His own, they are announcing their defiance of Him. The issue is then between God and the enemy. We can be sure that He will bring them to account.

We must understand that it is not important whether or not we see the process turn full circle. We can rest in absolute confidence—God will do all that needs to be done. Our Lord is competent. With this knowledge we can rest!

We Will Possess

The method by which God moved to meet Jephthah's personal need is worthy of expanded comment. More than with either of the aforementioned judges, the man himself is in evidence. He looked his former detractors in the face as they sued for his help. When the rejected outcast heard them say, "Come, and be our captain . . . be our head over all the inhabitants of Gilead" (Jud. 11:6, 8), it was not simply salve for his injured ego. It was the ingrafting of the divine estimate of his actual worth. This was Jehovah's means of preparing His chosen man to deal with the stern issues he would shortly confront.

Jephthah was now prepared to turn to the enemy. He methodically identified the rightness of Israel's claim to the disputed territory. There is a ring of iron confidence as he offered the Ammonites an ultimatum without compromise. There would be no negotiations. "So whomsoever the LORD our God shall drive out from before us, them will we possess"

(Jud. 11:24). No question about it, he believed God! He was not living under the intimidating remorse of being a harlot's son; he was standing in the power of a delivering God.

We might well pause and ask ourselves how we stack up when we stand before our old and persistent enemies. Do we have the kind of confidence that thunders "we will possess"?

At this juncture, inspiration records, "Then the Spirit of the LORD came upon Jephthah" (Jud. 11:29). Now it was the enemy who had to defend his position. Divine enablement had assured human victory. The combat would be hand to hand and eyeball to eyeball. Blood would flow, but the enemy would flee or fall. This type of resounding victory would supply all of the spiritual mettle necessary for Jephthah's future days of leadership. God had demonstrated His love, favor, and power in unmistakable fashion. Oh yes, we can be sure that there were still those slinkingly secretive character assassins who snickered about his parentage—the Devil saw to that. But we can be equally certain that their snide comments were made in hushed whispers behind securely closed doors.

"So Jephthah passed over unto the children of Ammon to fight against them; and the LORD delivered them into his hands" (Jud. 11:32). Jephthah exercised obedience in crossing over to face the enemy, and Jehovah accomplished what He promised. "He smote them . . . with a very great slaughter. Thus the children of Ammon were subdued before the children of Israel" (Jud. 11:33). The harlot's son became a judge in Israel and in so doing took his place alongside the ancient heroes of the people of God.

The Outgrowth Problem

Jephthah was no more immune to problems in victory than were his predecessors. In his case, the problem centered in his famous vow. In our consideration of his difficulties, it is necessary to look at three things.

117

The Impulsiveness of His Vow

"And Jephthah vowed a vow unto the LORD" (Jud. 11:30). Vows in the Old Testament were permitted as a wholly voluntary practice. They usually consisted of a promise to God to perform some service in return for Jehovah's aid. Making a vow was regarded as very solemn, and it was not to be practiced capriciously or without the most serious forethought. "Be not rash with thy mouth, and let not thine heart be hasty to utter any thing before God" (Eccl. 5:2). Jesus roundly condemned those who abused their vows (see Mt. 5:33-37).

Jephthah's vow was as unnecessary as it was regrettable. It was unnecessary because he already had the assurance of victory, and he knew it. We observed this in our consideration of Judges 11:24, which said, "So whomsoever the LORD our God shall drive out from before us, them will we possess." The power of God was already clearly upon him for the accomplishment of the task at hand: "Then the Spirit of the LORD came upon Jephthah" (Jud. 11:29). His vow, therefore, became a bit of added insurance that offered his sincerity to God as additional collateral for the coming victory. It was certainly, at the time, a well-intended act of piety. But in the final analysis we must position it alongside Gideon's fleece as both inane and superfluous.

Victories for God are never won or assisted by our capacity for striking bargains with omnipotence. Those of us who aspire to be modern *Jephthahs* must learn this! Victories come through our *believing* and *obeying* divine dictates. They are not brought to pass by fits of pious promise made during periods of emotional elation or circumstantial duress. This is in no way intended to minimize our Lord's activity in bringing His people to the place of basic yielding or the forsaking of individual sins through His chastisement. It is intended to expose the fallacy of asking God to do something for us in return for our giving up something we should not be doing anyway.

For example, it is totally wrong for a Christian to promise to tithe if God will, in return, pay the bills and make the believer at least comfortably well-to-do in the process. It is equally abhorrent for preachers to appeal to their people by pressing the same motivation. Indeed, they may find themselves in the position of a minister who was hauled into court by a couple who alleged that the pastor promised them wealth if they would begin to tithe to his church. They did not become wealthy, so they turned on the well-meaning culprit, charging that his promise had been fraudulent. Christians should give to the Lord's work because it is right to give. If we go to the poorhouse in the process, it is still right to obey God in the matter of our giving.

In the same vein, how many ministers have stood by hospital beds and heard well-intentioned saints make countless promises to give up sinful habits and begin to be faithful to the Lord and His church if God would only raise them up from the bed of suffering? We wince when we think of how few of these plaintive petitioners actually remember the Lord or their fervent promises when He mercifully allows them to recover. Deity does not invite a Christian to negotiate what he should do, on the promise of some special concession on His part. We are commanded to yield everything to Him— yield in the confidence that His victories will be ours, yield in spite of what adversity may follow. There is a needed lesson to be learned here: Our shallow promise-making must be replaced by an abiding yieldedness to His will and work.

The Vow

"Then it shall be, that whatsoever cometh forth of the doors of my house to meet me, when I return in peace from the children of Ammon, shall surely be the LORD's, and I will offer it up for a burnt offering" (Jud. 11:31). This vow has been the source of great controversy and debate. Many commentators feel that Jephthah actually sacrificed his daughter who was the first to meet him when he returned from the battle. This idea must be rejected on the basis of both simple reason and biblical evidence.

First, we must understand that Jephthah was a genuine worshiper of Jehovah. He was not some near-heathen bumpkin. He was well acquainted with the Word of God and the practices of true worship. There were few things more noxious to the mind of a pious Jew than the prospect of human sacrifice. Even in the event that someone did wish it done, who would do it? Certainly not a priest of Israel. Where would it be accomplished? Most assuredly not at the Tabernacle in Shiloh. No, it seems that we can reject any thought of this on the grounds of reason alone.

However, there are also some sound biblical keys available to us. The words, as rendered in the New American Standard Version, indicate, "it shall be the LORD's, *or* I will offer it up as a burnt offering." Both possibilities seem to have been considered. If it is human, it shall be the Lord's. On the other hand, if it is an animal, it will be offered as a burnt offering. Jephthah was paralyzed with regret when he saw his only daughter come to meet him "with timbrels and with dances" (Jud. 11:34). This child was the love of his life. Her act indicated that she, too, loved her father very deeply. Joy was turned into weeping, and the festive air became one of mourning, as the battle-weary Gileadite "tore his clothes" (Jud. 11:35) in demonstration of abject remorse.

But, alas, the vow so rashly made must now painfully be served. Both father and daughter would be affected for life. Her request, subsequent to the revelation of the vow of her father, is significant. She requested time to "go up and down upon the mountains, and bewail my virginity" (Jud. 11:37). Her lament was not over the prospect of her life being terminated but over the prospect of perpetual virginity. Verse 39 notes, "and she knew no man." This leads us to observe rather conclusively that she was given to perpetual virginity and service to Jehovah, perhaps at the Tabernacle in Shiloh.

More darkness is thrown over the lamentable scene. "And she was his only child; beside her he had neither son nor daughter" (Jud. 11:34). Jephthah would never have an heir! His daughter would not be alone in bewailing her virginity; Jephthah would lament his impetuous act for the remainder of his life.

The Implications of His Vow

Jephthah had been treated with cruelty and gross injustice by his brothers and the townspeople. He had been forced to bear the consequences of an act of which he was completely innocent. Others decided his fate and condemned him to it, whether or not he agreed to it. Then he did precisely the same thing to his own daughter. He made the vow, and she was thus committed to a fate in which she had no voice, other than her consent to obey. It became her lot to suffer the consequences of her father's ill-advised act.

How often this happens to the best of us. Satan seems to take great delight in maneuvering us into positions where we impose on others the very things that have been great sources of trial to us. Often we are guilty of expecting people to live by the standards we set for them, while we forget how we chafed under impositions we felt to be unfair in bygone days.

Parents often make the mistake of attempting, without explanation, to impose things upon their children that they themselves ridiculed and resented when their parents did the same to them. Unfortunately, the most injurious impositions seem to be associated with restrictions or requirements totally unrelated to essential biblical standards. Young Christians, too, are frequently plagued by those who know all about how they ought to live but have forgotten how it was with them in the infancy of their own Christian experience.

The Remedy

We can quickly conclude that, as with the judges already studied, we are all affected to some degree by Jephthah's outgrowth problem. The remedy can best be summarized in the word *reservation*—reservation regarding our tendency to be hasty with our words. We must learn to think before we speak and to be certain, as much as possible, that what we promise, propose, or promote is in the will of God and will accomplish constructive spiritual ends.

Some of us seem to be in perpetual trouble because of a tendency to think with our mouths. Ill-advised words, written or spoken, often create bad situations and fractured friendships. Abraham Lincoln's practice of writing in anger and then placing those letters in drawers until he cooled off is an admirable pattern to follow. The objective is, of course, to communicate clearly after ample time for thought, analysis, and careful reflection.

James admonished us to be "swift to hear, slow to speak" (Jas. 1:19). Between the hearing and the speaking lies a practice that has nearly expired of neglect. It is meditation. The notion has been all but monopolized by the proponents of Eastern cultic mysticism. This does not, however, minimize its importance to modern-day Christians. We need to reawaken our understanding of the importance of spending time in quiet meditation. Consider the words of the Psalmist: "Let the words of my mouth, and the meditation of my heart, be acceptable in thy sight, O LORD, my strength, and my redeemer" (Ps. 19:14). Again in Psalm 77:12 the Word records, "I will meditate also of all thy work, and talk of thy doings." In the New Testament, Timothy was told, after having been instructed concerning the development of his ministry gifts, to "Meditate upon these things" (1 Tim. 4:15).

The word *meditation* carries the idea of pondering, reflecting upon, weighing mentally, considering carefully, and deliberating. Our Lord spent extended periods of time alone in communion with His Father. These interludes were given to prayer and meditation—reflecting upon the labors of the coming day and the larger tasks that lay before Him in Jerusalem. Meditation was very much a part of His preparation for the great work of redemption.

Some of us have great difficulty developing a meditative spirit because it takes time, something we simply do not have much of these days. We feel that we must do quickly whatever we are currently occupied with. Devotional guides are available to enable people to compress daily communion with the Lord into a few moments snatched hurriedly during the rush of preparation for the day. Devotional exercises frequently consist of a short reading, a short comment, and a short prayer. We are incessantly in a hurry about practically everything we do. Why? "The tempo of life," we say. By whose design? God's or Satan's?

Let's think about that question for a moment. Have you noticed what has taken place in the past few years? The entire structure of contemporary life seems to be increasingly geared toward ensuring that we are distracted from extended, serious reflection on the things of God. This is the age of *noise!* Everywhere we turn, there it is. The sound of radio throbs through supermarkets, doctors' waiting rooms, and automobiles. Young people stab at lesson preparation to the accompaniment of earsplitting renditions repeated interminably on cassette players. The pale luminescence of the television screen illuminates homes from sun up until the wee hours, so dominating household activities it is often difficult to carry on a conversation or enjoy a visit with friends. Even in our houses of worship, we are assaulted by wall-shaking vibrations designed, it seems, to shatter windows and kill vegetation for miles around—and in the name of music.

The counterpart of noise is that aforementioned culprit, hurry. We whirl through exhausting days at breakneck speed. Time is always of the essence. Priorities are established on a crisis basis—whatever squeaks loudest gets fleeting attention. Life has become, for many, a patchwork of emergency treatments. There is little time for doing much of anything with deliberation and thoroughness.

The conclusions, we think, are quite obvious. For the worldling, the design is to divert the mind from occupation with the stern issues of life and death, thereby minimizing the possibility of giving serious thought to the need for Christ. With the combination of the elements already mentioned and the addition of our addiction to multitudinous forms of entertainment, it is possible for a person to live out his days with his mind totally dominated every waking moment by distracting influences. For the believer, the program is fashioned to deprive us of a clear vision of God's purpose for our lives. It is further designed to strip us of our personal power with God.

Admittedly, dealing with this grim tyrant is no small matter. But the determination of the enemy to resist our efforts of effective communion only emphasizes the necessity of our triumphing in the matter. However we achieve it, we must have adequate opportunity to hear our God, ponder carefully what He is saying to us, and then converse unhurriedly with Him in prayer.

Here is a suggested structure for devotional activity, giving place for the three essential ingredients for successful communion.

1. Time with the *Word*: Devotional books are good; however, we must encounter God's written Word firsthand and allow it to speak directly to our receptive hearts and minds.

2. Time for reflection and *meditation*: Program a period designed to open the mind to the prompting of the Holy Spirit and take time to ponder carefully what He has revealed through the Word. Also, ruminate on the problems currently confronting you and spend some time expecting and awaiting divine guidance. You will be amazed at how often decisions and problems are settled during such periods of sanctified interaction between the Word, the Holy Spirit, and a submissive believer. These moments of meditation can offer immeasurable assistance in avoiding Jephthah's pitfall of making hasty and ill-advised decisions.

3. Time for *prayer*: Asking, giving thanks, and seeking direction assume a new perspective when we approach the throne after a period of meditation. We believe that the Spirit prays for us; we must also concede that He delights in directing our minds toward those things that are of compelling importance in our Christian living.

Yes, this process does require time. We may find varying intervals that we, as individuals, can invest. However, we must ask ourselves this question: Can we afford not to *make* time for propositions of such overwhelming importance? Certainly we must. Each of us should review our own schedules and commitments and then set aside a time uniquely adaptable to our own situation. It will prove to be a wise investment.

Dr. J. Sidlow Baxter and I were discussing devotional practices one day. He suggested a marvelous method for devotional interaction with the Lord and His Word. "Take a book," he advised, "say, one of the epistles. Read each verse slowly and carefully. If there is a word of admonition, stop for a moment, asking the Lord to make that admonition real in your life. If it is a warning, pause to meditate on the importance of that warning. Should a praise note rise, join in with praise to your Heavenly Father. In this way you can pray and praise your way through the entire Word of God."

Dr. Baxter's method has stood me in good stead for years. I'm sure it can do the same for you.

6

SAMSON—The Failure

SAMSON

Born of promise, prayer, and fire,
    A Nazirite he entered
To rout the loathsome Philistines
    With strength Jehovah-centered.

But few among the sons of men
    Who came God's place to fill,
Have fallen to such depths of woe
    As Samson at the mill.

With sightless eyes and shaven head
    We see him grinding there,
He proves again the price that's paid
    To eat the devil's fare.

He prays with hands on columns tall
    In childlike eloquence.
The lesson, late but learned, is his—
    FAITH and OBEDIENCE.

And there was a certain man of Zorah, of the family of the Danites, whose name was Manoah; and his wife was barren, and bore not. And the angel of the LORD appeared unto the woman, and said unto her, Behold, now, thou art barren, and bearest not; but thou shalt conceive, and bear a son. Now, therefore, beware, I pray thee, and drink not wine nor strong drink, and eat not any unclean thing. For, lo, thou shalt conceive, and bear a son; and no razor shall come on his head; for the child shall be a Nazirite unto God from the womb. And he shall begin to deliver Israel out of the hand of the Philistines. Then the woman came and told her husband, saying, A man of God came unto me, and his countenance was like the countenance of an angel of God, very awesome; but I asked him not from where he was, neither told he me his name (Jud. 13:2–6).

But the Philistines took him, and put out his eyes, and brought him down to Gaza, and bound him with fetters of bronze; and he did grind in the prison house. Howbeit, the hair of his head began to grow again after he was shaved (Jud. 16:21–22).

And Samson called unto the LORD, and said, O Lord GOD, remember me, I pray thee, and strengthen me, I pray thee, only this once, O God, that I may be at once avenged of the Philistines for my two eyes. And Samson took hold of the two middle pillars upon which the house stood, and on which it was borne up, of the one with his right hand, and of the other with his left. And Samson said, Let me die with the Philistines. And he bowed himself with all his might; and the house fell upon the lords, and upon all the people who were in it. So the dead whom he slew at his death were more than they whom he slew in his life (Jud. 16:28–30).

F EW MEN HAVE ENTERED the earthly scene with more impressive credentials than did Samson. Events surrounding his birth place him alongside those who were *born of promise*. As we scan the early record of his life, we immediately experience a surge of expectancy. The feeling mounts that great things must be in store as the life of this exceptional individual begins to unfold. But, alas, only bewildering disappointment awaits the reader as he witnesses an historic example of lost opportunities and squandered potential.

Samson's Birth

Samson's impending birth was heralded by an angelic ambassador. He was born into a truly godly family. Furthermore, he was to be a "Nazirite unto God from the womb" (Jud. 13:5). Coupled with these facts is the revelation of Jehovah's purpose for Samson: "He shall *begin* to deliver Israel out of the hand of the Philistines" (Jud. 13:5). The initial accounts of his deeds relate how he was strengthened and moved by the Spirit of God. We can say without hesitation that our subject was a man set apart by God to accomplish extraordinary things. Scriptures related to his life give at least five evidences of this.

1. *The Angel's Announcement:* "And the angel of the LORD appeared unto the woman, and said unto her, Behold, now, thou art barren, and bearest not; but thou shalt conceive, and bear a son" (Jud. 13:3). This was quite possibly a visitation by none other than our Lord Jesus Christ Himself in a preincarnate appearance. The angel of the Lord came to the barren wife of a Danite, Manoah, with the news that she would bear a son. Upon His departure Manoah declared, "we have seen God" (Jud. 13:22). This visitation is of compelling interest, particularly because of the range of detail and instruction to the parents regarding the child. In addition, the Lord took care to verify that the visit was of great consequence by demonstrating His power as "the angel did wondrously, [while] Manoah and his wife looked on" (Jud. 13:19). This was to be the same power that would course through the body of Samson, who was sent to begin to deliver Israel from the Philistines.

2. *Samson's Parents:* Manoah and his wife had suffered under the oppression of the Philistines. Along with other pious Jews, they had doubtless prayed that Jehovah would give them a child through whom He might show His power. Like Hannah, Mary, and numerous others in Scripture, they gave themselves to petitioning Heaven that their offspring might be signally used of God for some great work. How fortunate are those who can claim praying parents whose deepest yearnings are for the Lord to use their children.

Not only were they *praying* parents, but these people wished sincerely to know how to teach their coming son. Manoah's prayer illustrates the point: "O my Lord, let the man of God whom thou didst send come again unto us, and teach us what we shall do unto the child that shall be born" (Jud. 13:8). He further requested insight as to what the baby's vocation was to be: "How shall we order the child, and how shall we do unto him?" (Jud. 13:12).

Clearly, they sought *guidance* that they might be *taught* to properly direct the young deliverer in preparation for his appointed tasks. They requested to know the Lord's name that "we may do thee honor" (Jud. 13:17). Certainly this gives a wealth of insight into their heart of hearts. They wanted to honor God in everything they were about. Their mission was to magnify Him by raising a child for His use.

We must pause here and make a point that seems lost to many in our generation. In the mad dash for self-fulfillment and acquisition of things, parenting—particularly mothering— has fallen into disrepute. Even in some Christian quarters, being a "non-career" type mother is viewed as a sort of second-class venture. Manoah and his saintly wife come before us as eloquent contradictions. They were people who were wholly given to the Lord; His priorities were theirs. At this juncture their highest priority was to raise this child to fulfill God's purposes. There was no priority, privilege, or pleasure on earth that could provide a richer reward.

3. *His Nazirite Position:* "For, lo, thou shalt conceive, and bear a son; and no razor shall come on his head; for the child shall be a Nazirite unto God from the womb" (Jud. 13:5). Two types of Nazirites are found in the Scriptures—temporary and perpetual. Those who took a temporary vow did so of their own volition for a stated period of time. Perpetual Nazirites were those who were such from their birth. Only three men— Samson, Samuel, and John the Baptist—bear this distinction.

A Nazirite was to be separated unto Jehovah. The word *nazir*, from which the word is probably derived, means *to separate.* As is always true, separation *to* God also involves separation *from* some things. Even some things that, in themselves, were perfectly acceptable for others were inappropriate for the Nazirite. Among specific details regarding the Nazirite, three are predominant. The hair was to go uncut (Jud. 13:5); he was to refrain from partaking of the fruit of the vine—no strong drink (Jud. 13:4); and contact with the dead was strictly forbidden.

Alfred Edersheim makes a very illuminating comment: "We have also here the idea of the royal priesthood, since the word nazir is applied to the holy crown upon the mitre of the high priest, and the 'crown of the anointing oil,' as also, in a secondary sense to the royal crown. We find, therefore, in the

Nazirite, the three ideas of separation, holiness, and the crown of the royal priesthood, all closely connected."

This helps to explain the great significance of Samson's hair. Of course, his strength was God-given. The emblems of Naziriteship were symbolic evidences of that enablement. They were outward testimony of being God's servant and were evidenced by his attire and conduct. He was separated (no contact with the dead), holy (abstaining from wine, which symbolized worldly joy as opposed to joy in Jehovah), and crowned (uncut hair).

The hair was the sign of his divine royalty—the chosen of God. He was to be God's voice, Israel's deliverer and judge. It was his crown and the mark that he was unique. When, through Delilah's wiles, he fell and the crafty Philistines snipped off his flowing locks, he was actually being deprived of his crown of testimony and separation. His witness was thus forfeited; his power with Jehovah was lost and fellowship with God was disrupted.

This is not something to be viewed as deeply mystical or complicated. Nor is it as superficial as unshorn hair. His loss of power was a result of his violation of firmly fixed principles in the economy of God. He had sunk successively lower in his distinction as a Nazirite before Delilah. In so doing, he forced God to remove his crown of power and testimony and fell prey to the dire consequences that were forthcoming.

4. *His Mission:* Jehovah revealed that he was to *begin* to deliver Israel from the Philistines' scourge. "And he shall begin to deliver Israel out of the hand of the Philistines" (Jud. 13:5). This seems to anticipate Samson's coming failure. He would leave the enemy badly crippled but still in control. Final victory would be left to someone else. He would not share Paul's exultant exclamation that he had completed his work: "I have fought a good fight, I have finished my course, I have kept the faith" (2 Tim. 4:7).

There is a sad note in this, for going home to Heaven with the Lord's business unfinished is a dismal prospect to contemplate. Each believer must be sobered by the thought that one day he will stand before the Lord to face the results of his earthly labors. "For we must all appear before the judgment seat of Christ, that everyone may receive the things done in his body, according to that he hath done, whether it be good or bad" (2 Cor. 5:10). At the judgment seat of Christ, each Christian will keep that appointment to meet the Lord and see his labors tested. Two great thoughts predominate: *reward* or *regret*.

The Scriptures clearly teach that those who are Christ's will never face a judgment in eternity to determine whether or not they are saved. We may reverently thank our Savior that judgment passed for us nearly two thousand years ago when Christ was judged in our place at Calvary. We will, however, have our earthly labors reviewed. "Every man's work shall be made manifest; for the day shall declare it, because it shall be revealed by fire; and the fire shall test every man's work of what sort it is" (1 Cor. 3:13). When our works are tested, we will be rewarded or suffer loss. Those who suffer loss will know an acute sense of regret as a result of bypassing the best in life spiritually, and witness before the Lord the ill-invested efforts of a lifetime go up in smoke.

5. *The Work of the Spirit:* "And the Spirit of the LORD began to move him at times" (Jud. 13:25). It is stated that Samson was moved upon by the Spirit of God on at least four occasions. This is more than is said of any other judge. With all of his marvelous physical attributes, he was, in the final analysis, totally dependent on the power of the Spirit of God. That he was chosen and empowered by the Lord was in itself a matter of great consequence.

The Philistines had oppressed Israel for 40 grueling years. This man was to be God's champion. On his shoulders was draped the mantle of divine approval and promise—so much so that when the Philistines paraded Goliath before the armies of Israel years later, it is believed they were actually fielding their long-sought answer to God's Samson. Jehovah had brought a man into this world and was now about to use him to punish His enemies, bless His people, and bring peace

137

to His land. All this would come by the hand of one human being. How little the champion thought of it. How sad to witness his failure to grasp the full import of what God had purposed to do through him.

Samson's Failure

How could Samson fail? He was a gifted, well-prepared, God-sent son of Abraham. But the glaring reality is this: He did! He fell as far as any child of God has ever fallen. The causes of his failure seem to be legion. As they stretch out over several pages of the Bible, they ring with a familiarity that is almost monotonous. We have seen all of these things take place over and over again. The distressing truth is that many of us have fallen to the same faults as our errant judge. He was afflicted by a number of problems.

The Failure To Listen

In the opening verses of Judges 14, we find Samson at odds with his parents over a Philistine woman. "Is there no woman among the daughters of thy brethren, or among all my people, that thou goest to take a wife of the uncircumcised Philistines?" (Jud. 14:3). But Samson said to his father, "Get her for me; for she pleaseth me well" (Jud. 14:3). We are then told that the parents did not realize that God was seeking an occasion against the Philistines (Jud. 14:4). However, it is doubtful that Samson knew it either, and it appears that God allowed Samson's choice in His permissive will. Samson dismissed the counsel of his godly parents without so much as the courtesy of an explanation beyond, "Get her for me; for she pleaseth me well." With this he embarked on a course that was clearly in opposition to the training of his parents and the instruction of the Word of God. He was determined to find his own way without guidance from others.

Samson saw his parents in the role of thing-getters. Do what I want—no questions asked. With him, as with an innumerable host who have followed in his wake, he was not open to criticism or direction from his parents. He would learn soon enough the price required for his intransigence.

We should pause here to offer some words of encouragement to those who, like Manoah and his wife, despair over the later failure of cherished offspring. We can only speculate about the nights passed in tearful supplication for their wayward boy. As far as we can ascertain, they cannot be faulted in their training of their son. They had done all God expected of them; they had been faithful. The fact is that occasionally children raised in the best Christian homes fail God, shame their parents, and fall far short of their God-given potential. Those who have suffered or are now suffering thus must be assured that, contrary to what some would have them believe, a child's failure cannot automatically be laid to the failure of his parents. That may in some instances be a contributing factor, but it is by no means a universal fact.

It is regrettable that so many Christian young people pass through a period of life when their parents seem unworthy of rudimentary consideration, but Samson was one who fell prey to that problem. From the standpoint of satanic strategy, we can easily see why this is true. During this early period, some of life's most enduring decisions are being made. Education, marriage, and vocation are all in the process of being decided. This is the time when wise counsel and mature experience are imperative. If Satan can foster a breakdown in communication, create defiance, and encourage rash actions designed to shock parents, he is delighted. "Getting even" with parents who "are trying to run my life" can be the costliest error of a lifetime. Those who have made these mistakes all too often look back over shattered lives and admit that dad and mom knew best after all.

So it was with Samson. His refusal to listen to parental advice cost him what no human being should have to pay. But he made his own bed, and it proved to be a foul place indeed.

The Failure To Pray

Going hand in hand with his refusal to listen to his parents was his disregard of prayer. Those who will not listen to parents are seldom found making inquiries of God. The record is barren of any account of Samson's engaging in serious prayer until he cried out prior to his final act against the Philistines (Jud. 16:28-30). After all, he was young and strong. His rippling biceps, brash courage, and quick wit supplied resources enough for any contingency. Why waste time seeking the will of God in prayer? The simple reply must be that all human resources, even those of the most gifted, when misdirected lead only to calamity.

Often we hear the lament, "But how can I know the will of God for my life?" As it is with *faith* and *obedience*, the answer is not as complicated as we make it out to be. Let us remember that God wants us to know His will. It is not something He is attempting to conceal, but rather something He wishes to reveal.

Following are four steps to finding the will of God.

1. *The Word of God*: God reveals Himself through His Word. It is here that we learn of His salvation. It is also through the Word that we learn of His will for these lives of ours. Our old adversary wages a relentless warfare against our consistent pursuit of serious study of the Book. This is particularly true of young people. (Anyone who has worked in youth camps and witnessed teenagers struggling through the time allotted for personal devotions can testify to the reality of the conflict.) The disciples found the will of God through companioning with our Lord. His counsel is just as available to us, as we companion with Him through openhearted, submissive Bible study.

2. *Prayer*: "Yet ye have not, because ye ask not" (Jas. 4:2). Our Savior instructed us to ask and expect an answer—not simply once or twice, but consistently, sincerely seeking His guidance, all the while placing the alternatives before Him and

awaiting His decision. Persistence is indispensable. As with reading God's Word, we are often distracted and frustrated in our prayer lives. We must learn to develop a discipline in prayer. The very intensity of the struggle evidences the importance of our succeeding. Press on in specific, expectant prayer.

3. *Availability*: It is here that multitudes run aground in seeking the will of God. We can hardly expect to find direction if we never allow ourselves to be exposed to opportunities and possible areas of service. Avoiding youth conferences, missionary meetings, and Christian life gatherings is a pretty effective way of missing the will of God. For example, most church members, both young people and adults, refuse to attend consistently the annual missions conferences in their church. Yet this is precisely where most missionaries have found the will of God for their lives. The same may be said of ministers, Christian teachers, and a host of others who are now happily plying the pathways of God's purpose for them. As they sat under the ministries of those who were actually involved in Christian work, God spoke to them.

This is how it has always been and, we must conclude, will always be. Churches that provide opportunities for their youth to visit mission fields, travel on evangelistic tours, and visit Christian colleges are making a wise investment. It is in these real-life situations that people most often find definite personal direction for their lives.

Conversely, it can also be said that those who consistently choose the theater, dance, and countless hours before the television are jeopardizing their futures in the cause of Christ. It is safe to assume that they will not find the will of God in the aforementioned places. It might further be ventured that young people who feel compelled to accept summer employment, thus passing by opportunities for exposure along the lines we have examined, are also in danger of missing the will of God. Working in order to purchase a car or buy some other nonessential items may not be worth the ultimate price some Christians are paying. A year spent at a Bible college, where an individual can squarely face this matter of the will of God, can be the best investment of a lifetime. The point is, we must place ourselves in a position where we can be exposed to what God wants of us.

4. *Entering Open Doors*: The next logical step in finding the will of God is to enter the open doors. It is in so doing that we test aptitudes and develop a feeling of assurance in what we are doing. Too many have fallen to the *No* syndrome when it comes to attempting anything they have not done before. How can we expect to know God's long-range will if we refuse to take the first step? No infant learns to walk until it learns to take steps—one at a time. Finally, it walks boldly and in a straight line. Perhaps the most practical aspect in finding the will of God can be expressed in this way: Do the right thing, right now. Doing the thing I should do in the short term inevitably leads to God's will for the long term.

We must learn that the greatest thing we can do for our children and youth is to provide opportunities for them to become involved in some type of Christian service. Too many of our youth programs are designed to entertain and serve the youth rather than to teach them to serve the Lord. Living for Christ is a serving business; consequently, we must learn to serve by taking opportunities provided for us. We may only guess at the number of people who would be excellent teachers and Christian workers had they learned to say, "Yes, I'll try," rather than "No, I can't."

There may be a rare exception from time to time, but if a Christian believer diligently pursues these simple steps, he will find the will of God.

The Failure To Control Fleshly Appetites

Sexual impurity was a prime cause of Samson's disastrous fall. The "lust of the eye" helped forge the chains that were the emblems of his failure. Samson "saw a woman . . . she [pleased him] well . . . Then went Samson to Gaza, and saw there an harlot, and went in unto her . . . afterward . . . he loved a woman in the valley of Sorek, whose name was Delilah" (Jud. 14:1, 3; 16:1, 4). So runs the sordid chronicle of his love life.

It was this sin, with its entanglements, that helped lift his crown of testimony, gouge out his eyes, bind him with chains, and bend his back to the mill. "But the Philistines took him, and put out his eyes, and brought him down to Gaza, and bound him with fetters of bronze; and he did grind in the prison house" (Jud. 16:21).

The unveiling of what unbridled passion can inflict is frightening to contemplate, but view it we must and expose it for what it actually is. Hollywood can produce its films blatantly glorifying sexual misconduct and draping acts like those of David and Bathsheba (2 Sam. 11-12) in tantalizing fable. The truth, however, leads chillingly to a murdered Uriah—killed by a king who was trying to conceal his iniquity. Still further along is the pallid corpse of an infant victimized by his parents' lust. The lament of a frenzied Bathsheba, who suffered far more than the fleeting moments of illicit pleasure could ever compensate, testifies of the real "wages" sin delivers. David bowed in disgrace before the accusing finger of a distraught prophet as he was exposed before a nation. Furthermore, Israel's king was singled out for ridicule by the enemies of God, who thereafter felt justified in blaspheming the name of Jehovah because of his transgression: "Howbeit, because by this deed thou hast given great occasion to the enemies of the LORD to blaspheme" (2 Sam. 12:14). These are the true results of bowing to the flesh and allowing it to run rampant.

History sings a recurring dirge over disgraced ministers, weeping congregations, shattered homes, embittered children, crushed parents, and lost testimonies—all because individuals somehow came to believe that they could take fire to their breast and not be burned (Prov. 6:27). We must deplore the current flippancy in sexual matters that is invading our churches. The frequency of modern dereliction does not negate the divine injunctions against fornication, adultery, and impure

143

conduct. Perhaps no other single device in the arsenal of Satan holds out greater promise of satisfaction yet delivers more stupefying bondage. Sadly, all too many of our contemporaries grind out their spiritual lives with eyes gouged out and chained to the mill as they fall beneath the lash of remorse and anguished repentance.

The Failure To Be Consistent

As though the foregoing problems were not enough, we find that Samson was plagued by inconsistency. This may, in reality, be the key to his most basic problem. His spiritual life approximated a roller coaster, marked by mystifying extremes. He plunged from the summit to the depths with astounding regularity and rapidity. One moment he was knee deep in Philistines, soundly thrashing them with the Spirit of the Lord upon him (Jud. 15:15); the next moment he was at the harlot's door or draped on the lap of the sultry Delilah. He seemed to run more on emotion than on the application of sound, godly principles. In other words, he lacked basic spiritual discipline. This proved to be his most persistent and vexing problem.

The teaching and guidance lavished upon this favored leader by his parents and by the Lord Himself apparently went unheeded. Samson certainly had been instructed in every element of doctrine and preferred conduct. His tragedy was his persistent failure to apply what he had learned. For Samson, physical prowess and heated activity displaced spiritual dependence. Samson's strength apparently caused God's champion to begin looking in the wrong direction—to his own resources rather than the Lord's.

We may not run to Samson's violent extremes, but many among us must confess to great highs and lows, too often sharing Samson's proclivity toward extremes dictated largely by our emotions. This is one of the serious dangers involved in some of the current movements that put a great deal of emphasis on experience and sharing. The whirl of activity involved when we surround ourselves with *turned on* activists makes for heady sensations. But when the noise subsides and the mundane reality of life, with its round of duties and disappointments, presses in, depression can quickly take the place of exuberance. The solution to the problem is *consistency* in every area of Christian growth.

Central to all is learning the great doctrines of the Word and then applying them. *There is no substitute for this!* Slogans, bumper stickers, one-way signs, smiley buttons, and syncopated gospel music are not legitimate substitutes for sound doctrine. Let it be firmly stated that the studied superficiality of some of our modern groups is a major factor in the development of heretical elements proliferating in evangelical circles today. The current rush toward "contemporary" worship styles in the hope of creating more spiritual dynamics in our services can end in disaster. While creativity and innovation can be positive factors, true spiritual dynamics is not a created style, and what may appear to bring more life into a worship service may, in the end, distract congregations from the real sources of spiritual power.

Stability can come only through exercising proper discipline. It is impossible to be undisciplined and stable at the same time. This was Samson's great failure; it can also be ours. We must determine to learn and apply God's truth. There is no practical shortcut. Novel, innovative methods may offer great promise, but, in the cold light of eventual results, these methods in themselves will be found wanting.

The Failure To Properly Regard God's Gifts

Samson took God for granted! He came to believe that God's strength was his own personal possession. He felt that the Lord was obligated to bless him, in spite of his lack of faithfulness. Furthermore, he believed that it was unthinkable for Jehovah to allow him to fall into the hands of his enemies. He was proven wrong on all counts. God relieved him of his strength, withdrew His blessing, and summarily delivered him into the hands of the avowed enemies of Israel and the Lord. What a sad spectacle. God's champion was reduced to a compounder of riddles wagering for changes of clothing (Jud. 14:5-20). The source of his strength was the subject of untruthful exchanges with Delilah, who was clearly dedicated to his destruction. His ultimate sacrilege was demonstrated by his disclosure of the source of his strength to an enemy of his God: "he told her all his heart, and said unto her, There hath not come a razor upon mine head; for I have been a Nazirite unto God from my mother's womb: if I am shaved, then my strength will go from me, and I shall become weak, and be like any other man" (Jud. 16:17).

How could he do it? How could this man, so singularly blessed, with such wonderful beginnings, fall so far? Apparently Samson believed it just couldn't happen to him. He felt he could somehow play by another set of rules.

The sin to which men incline after God has brought great blessing upon them is usually this sin of regarding His blessing as obligatory and perpetual. When indulged in, it is sure to effect the same results as befell the hapless Nazirite.

The experiences of some of our great denominations and movements illustrate this process. Born in the flush of giant outpourings of the power of God, they surge forward with impressive success. The working of the Holy Spirit through submissive men and women triggers large floods of people seeking to share the blessings being experienced by movements evidencing the blessing and power of God. Yet, in the process of time, organization replaces unction. Large bank accounts supplant dependence on the provision of God in direct answer to prayer. Impressive structures and intricate rituals become substitutes for the compelling attraction of the gospel message. Finally, the institutions of learning begin to emphasize academic excellence and expression to the extent that meeting human standards turns them from their founding purposes. Reliance upon the teaching ministry of the Holy Spirit becomes an outmoded and often ridiculed proposition. It is all depressingly familiar and should certainly cause us to see the signs as ensigns of warning.

Conservative Christians often reassure each other that this cannot happen to us. After all, we are true to God. We should take note that almost without exception the groups and institutions that we now regard as liberal and apostate once stood as bastions of biblical truth. They thought it would never happen to them—but it did! And it will as surely happen to some of the current crop of conservatives unless the warning signals are heeded.

We must all learn that we cannot violate scriptural principles and remain immune to serious spiritual problems. An arresting example of this process comes to mind. Some years ago, a man who had been a notorious alcoholic was gloriously converted to Christ. His immediate deliverance from the powers of drink was a joy to those who had known and prayed for him over the years. His testimony was radiant, and his eagerness to serve the Lord engendered admiration among the members of the Christian community.

One day he approached his pastor with what he considered exciting news. "I've been going back into the bars where I spent so many wasted hours, sitting down with my former cronies, and witnessing to them." His pastor had serious reservations. "I feel you are making a serious error in returning to the bars," he counseled. "The principle is that we are to avoid potential sources of temptation, particularly in areas of known weakness, such as yours with alcohol." "Now pastor," came the impatient reply, "you need not worry. I know what I'm doing. Everything will be all right."

A few weeks later the pastor entered the man's home in response to an urgent call from his wife. The brother so recently delivered was drunk. He sat on the bed cross-legged, with tears of regret coursing down his cheeks. "Oh preacher, I've made an awful mess of things. You warned me, but I wouldn't listen. The very thing you feared might happen did."

The strength of that man's witness was compromised because he felt he was something special. In his mind, he did not need to fear a fall if he failed to exercise sound spiritual judgment. Like Samson, he was wrong, and recovery was a slow and painful process.

Samson's calamity is chronicled in Judges 16. The words pierce like arrows as they fall from the pages of Scripture. "And his strength went from him . . . And he knew not that the LORD was departed from him" (Jud. 16:19-20). Here, then, is the irony of it: He went on, not knowing that he no longer possessed divine strength, and persisted until he was overcome by his own impotence. Being an abject spiritual failure, yet moving on as though all was well, was his tragic state. "But the Philistines took him, and put out his eyes, and brought him down to Gaza, and bound him with fetters of bronze; and he did grind in the prison house" (Jud. 16:21).

Favorite Bible verses are often displayed by Christians as reminders of promises our Lord has given us. Perhaps when we are on the verge of failure, it would be well to have available verses that illustrate the dire consequences of defections from the pathway of simple obedience.

We could linger here and pry open other corners of our subject's failure to achieve what God had purposed for him. However, it is far better for us to turn with relief to his recovery.

The Remedy

"Howbeit, the hair of his head began to grow again after he was shaved" (Jud. 16:22). More was growing for Samson than the hair on his head. Although this is one of those silent areas about which we must restrict our considerations to sanctified speculation, we can be certain that the Holy Spirit was working with quiet effectiveness over His servant.

The shame and humiliation he was forced to endure must have laid heavily on Samson. As he ground in wearying repetition at the mill, his mind must have been filled with memories of what used to be. Philistines falling and fleeing at the sight of him, the surge of divine strength filling his being, crowds of Israelites waiting before him to be judged and counseled, the balmy days of being a household word among God's chosen people—all must have passed repeatedly through his mind. Augmenting these memories were haunting scenes of the lust-filled misadventures that finally served to bring him low. It was as he saw his life from the perspective of a prisoner that his values took a monumental turn. He finally grasped the truth that his former strength was actually not his own, but only what a beneficent God had bestowed upon him. Samson began to learn the lessons of applied prayer and humility before Jehovah. He came to a place of functional belief—that is, to truly believe God about himself (Samson) and his God. The process of faith and obedience was set in motion.

"And Samson called unto the LORD, and said, O Lord GOD, remember me, I pray thee, and strengthen me, I pray thee, only this once" (Jud. 16:28). For the first time in the story of Samson, he reflected a sense of inadequacy and true humility before God. He was ready to accept death rather than live out his days in shamefaced defeat and servitude.

The difference between Samson and so many modern-day Christians is dramatically accentuated at this point. He was willing to do something about his condition.

Note the process:

"Samson called unto the LORD" (Jud. 16:28). Bound up in this statement was his willingness to *confess* his sinfulness and need of divine forgiveness.

"O Lord GOD, remember me" (Jud. 16:28). Manifested here is a desire for the restoration of *fellowship* with God.

"Let me die with the Philistines" (Jud. 16:30). In this can be seen the great proposition of *death to self*.

"He bowed himself with all his might" (Jud. 16:30). Samson applied himself to *positive involvement* in what little remained of his life.

The remedy came in a thoroughgoing transformation. If any person in history could have felt justified in pleading that it was too late, it was Samson. He appeared to have fallen so far and disgraced himself so completely that no possibility of redeeming service was left for him. But this was no more true for Samson than for the reader of these lines who feels so badly lacerated by defeat that he sees no point in becoming spiritually involved again.

We meet so many people who view the past with tearful nostalgia but feel that they can never rise again. Samson found that Jehovah was the God of the *failure* too!

> The night can bring
>   No darker thought
> Than that within
>   The failure wrought.
>
> Who wreaths a family,
>   Friend and name
> With emblems of
>   Some public shame.
>
> Would cause to wonder
>   If could be,
> One such could e'er
>   Forgiveness see?
>
> Now hear the word
>   Direct and true:
> "I'm Savior of
>   The failure too."
>
> Then quit the place
>   Of dark remorse,
> To find in Christ
>   Life's future course.

What a revelation it must have been. He had every reason to think that God had turned His back in righteous disgust and would never look toward him again. If Samson had such thoughts, he badly underestimated the grace and mercy of his Lord. Yes, he paid an extremely high price for his misconduct. He even died prematurely as a result. However, he passed the portals of paradise possessing the assurance of the greatness of a God who allowed him to return to the place of blessing and victory before taking leave of the earthly scene.

Look again at the steps we must apply in recovering from our backsliding. *Confession* evidences a willingness to agree with God about the nature and consequences of sin. In this we at once deal decisively with pride or rebellion and the habit of shrinking from exposure that hinders us from making a clean breast of our dereliction. Confession also has a public element about it. Sins that are committed publicly must be confessed publicly. Offenses against Christian brothers, churches, family members, and loved ones must be righted, insofar as is humanly possible. This is a great stumbling stone in the return of many. Again, the root of the problem is misguided pride. In addition to this, many people tend to underestimate the willingness of those who love Christ to forgive and forget. Often years of frustration and enmity are ended the moment one takes affirmative action to right wrongs.

Fellowship is the return to a realization of the abiding presence of Christ and the development of a deepening love for Him as Savior and Lord. This is the key to going on with God. Many of us make the mistake of viewing the Christian life and separated living as a set of rules and prohibitions that become impersonal and restrictive. When this occurs, it is virtually certain that we will either become cold legalistic Pharisees or despair over our inability to perform up to standard.

Christ is the basis of everything in the Christian life, just as a wife or husband is the basis of married life. Life is a relationship. Relating to people tempers all of the vehicles for living in the day to day. With believers this is magnified ten thousandfold. Fellowship with Christ is our motivation, pleasure, purpose, and fulfilment. Separation *from* the world must always begin with our separation *to* Him.

Death to self then becomes a viable possibility. Only as we discover life in someone else can we find just cause to die to self. We simply offer up our lives to Him. Death to self becomes the logical and normal thing to do.

Finding self-esteem has been high on the Christian priority list for some time now. Actually, the way to the thing Christians profess to be looking for begins with death to self. "I am crucified with Christ: nevertheless I live; yet not I, but Christ liveth in me; and the life which I now live in the flesh I live by the faith of the Son of God, who loved me and gave himself for me" (Gal. 2:20). Christ-esteem is the only legitimate life expression of the redeemed.

Positive involvement is the natural outgrowth of confession, fellowship, and death to self. It is also essential to our continuing victory. As we are possessed with Christ, we are also occupied with knowing His will and doing it. This is the abiding formula. "And Samson took hold of the two middle pillars upon which the house stood, and on which it was borne up, of the one with his right hand, and of the other with his left. And Samson said, Let me die with the Philistines. And he bowed himself with all his might; and the house fell upon the lords, and upon all the people who were in it. So the dead whom he slew at his death were more than they whom he slew in his life" (Jud. 16:29–30).

The Lord heard Samson and strengthened him to accomplish the task at hand. In the same process, He vindicated His name and crippled the Philistines by the destruction of their leaders, who were in attendance at the affair.

Not only did God emerge victorious over the enemy and accomplish a stunning victory, but He exposed the foolish notion that Dagon (their god) had triumphed. As a matter of fact, Jehovah also destroyed the fallacious notion that it was Dagon who had delivered Samson into the hands of the Philistines. No, indeed, it was the Lord who had delivered him into their hands to bring about two clear objectives. First, they were employed by God as the instruments through which He would correct His wayward child. Those who are familiar with the Old Testament record recall that this was often the method God used to correct Israel. For example, Nebuchadnezzar was the chosen vessel through whom God chastised the Jewish people (see Hab. 1).

Behind all the struggles of the earthly sphere is the central conflict between God and Satan, a conflict in which it might appear that our adversary is having the best of it in this world. But while evil seems to be in the ascendancy and the ungodly triumph and prosper, we still hear the familiar, *Our god hath delivered into our hands.* The world loves to mock and scorn the saints and press as evidence the proposition that Christians are often a suffering lot, oppressed and trodden down. Their particular joy seems to be ridiculing those who have failed God and appear to be at the mercy of the world.

They fail to recognize, however, that they are often being used by God to exercise discipline over believers in need of correction. The absolute rule of the divine economy is that evil never ultimately triumphs. Prevailing wickedness is sooner or later turned into a testimonial to God's sovereign power and purposes in grace toward His people. As the Philistines rejoiced over a blinded Samson, they failed to realize that Jehovah was marking their godless belligerence and would soon call them to account for their wanton cruelty.

Thus, we see that all rebellion and godlessness will one day be recompensed. The transgressor eventually bears the responsibility for his iniquitous actions. In the process, God puts down the sinner and his god, which is actually a victory over Satan. Human history is replete with examples of this process. The aforementioned Babylonians are a clear example of this. After they had been used to chastise Jehovah's people, the stroke of divine judgment fell on them, and they passed into history. The same was true of the Philistines. Samson's last act was the beginning of the end for them. After they had served their purpose in the life of Samson, they were ground into an ignominious heap. What was to be their hour of great triumph became a death knell sounding over them. Would that all men and nations could see this principle. "So the dead whom he slew at his death were more than they whom he slew in his life" (Jud. 16:30).

The Outgrowth Problem

Samson experienced a peculiar yet common problem as a result of his restoration and final victory. He lingered in disobedience until his situation was so extreme that he faced a premature death. While we believe that, in the will of God, a Christian is immortal—that is, God will protect him until his appointed task on earth is fully accomplished—we must also believe that the disobedient Christian risks premature departure from life as a consequence of his refusal to repent and correct his conduct. The Word is clear concerning this. The Corinthians were admonished to approach the Lord's table with introspective self-examination. They had to face and forsake their sin lest they come into the situation described in 1 Corinthians 11:30: "For this cause many are weak and sickly among you, and many sleep [are dead]."

This condition is the most extreme evidence of God's corrective procedure with His children. It is, however, a very real consideration. When this occurs, we are faced with the same problem that Samson confronted. He waited so long to repent that when he finally did, he had no future left. He died forgiven, of course, but he exited bowed with stinging remorse over having no future ministry.

It is a solemn fact that the purpose for which we are created is to glorify and serve God. When we turn from this objective, we may justify our disobedience and rationalize our conduct until it seems unimportant whether or not we are spiritually productive. However, when we are right with Him, our thoughts immediately turn to service. Our joy is in being useful to God and His people. Those who delude themselves into thinking they can be satisfied with salvation although never occupied with service are in for a rude awakening. They join others who feel that carnality is a more pleasant way of life than earnest, sacrificial service. If they are truly Christians, they must realize what the Christ-life is really all about. It may not be until the waning years of life that true spiritual values begin to appear on the horizon of a life nearing eternity. It may be finally viewed from the vantage point of a deathbed experience, as one is embittered by remorse over lost opportunities. In any case, when we do see His purpose for us, we will have a deep longing to pass our days in service to Him.

Surveying a life of lost opportunities and an accumulation of spiritual debts that must go unpaid inevitably brings deep remorse to the heart and mind. Often we hear elderly people lament a youth spent pursuing self-interests. More distressing still is to see those who have committed themselves to Christ in the last stages of life longing for extended days in which to serve their Lord.

I was called on some years ago to visit a man afflicted by cancer. He was not aware that his disease was terminal. After I entered the room and introduced myself, I asked him if he was a Christian. He responded by saying that he was a member of a prominent church in the city.

"But that is not what I asked," I said.

He replied, "I know, but I didn't know what else to say."

"Would you like to know how to be assured of heaven?"

"Yes, if you can tell me, I would."

I proceeded to explain the way of salvation. He was intent on every word. After I finished, I asked, "Do you understand what I've said?"

"Yes, sir, I do."

"Would you like to accept Christ?"

"Yes, I would."

We bowed our heads, and he prayed an earnest simple prayer, confessing his sin and unworthiness and asking Christ to save him. I had prayer with him and then asked, "Are you saved?"

"Yes, I am!"

"How do you know?"

"Because I did what God asked me to do, and God did what He promised He would do."

For the few remaining weeks of his life my newfound fellow Christian was a radiant testimony for our Lord. He told everyone who came into his room about Christ. His family was amazed at the change that had taken place in his life. Those were wonderful days of blessing. They were also days of deep regret. As he began to grasp the fact that he would never leave that sickroom, he looked back to deplore a wasted life. He rejoiced at his assurance of Heaven, but there were so many needing Christ whom he could never reach. Many longtime believers are faced with the same plight when they come, in repentance, to have fellowship with Christ restored.

What is the remedy? Hear the word—*resolution*. Resolve to *do it now!* The only way one can avoid Samson's fate, no matter how badly he has erred, is to decide now, while there is still time, to get right with God, face honestly his failure, and be willing and eager to see his life made right.

Do it now! These words key every proposition faced in the lives of our specimen judges. Whether yours is a problem of facelessness, fear, being forsaken, or failure, begin to appropriate faith and practice obedience immediately. All the while remember that *with God there are no extraordinary people, only ordinary ones through whom He chooses to do extraordinary things.* You can be one of God's special *ordinary people!*